# HILLARY
# **CLINTON**

Look for more fascinating biographies in the series!

Sally Ride

Nelson Mandela

Steve Jobs

George W. Bush

Barack Obama

A REAL-LIFE STORY

# HILLARY
# CLINTON

AMERICAN WOMAN OF THE WORLD

by CHERYL HARNESS

**ALADDIN**

New York  London  Toronto  Sydney  New Delhi

ALADDIN

An imprint of Simon & Schuster Children's Publishing Division

1230 Avenue of the Americas, New York, New York 10020

First Aladdin hardcover edition July 2016

Text copyright © 2016 by Cheryl Harness

Front jacket photograph copyright © 2016 by Getty Images

Back jacket photograph copyright © 2016 by Getty Images

For information about special discounts for bulk purchases, please contact
Simon & Schuster Special Sales at 1-866-506-1949 or business@simonandschuster.com.

The Simon & Schuster Speakers Bureau can bring authors to your live event. For more
information or to book an event contact the Simon & Schuster Speakers Bureau at
1-866-248-3049 or visit our website at www.simonspeakers.com.

Book designed by Karina Granda

The text of this book was set in Bembo STD.

Manufactured in the United States of America 0616 FFG

2 4 6 8 10 9 7 5 3 1

Library of Congress Control Number 2016936303

ISBN 978-1-4814-6057-6 (hc)

ISBN 978-1-4814-6059-0 (eBook)

*For those who struggled for
women's full equality*

Women are the largest untapped reservoir of talent in the world.

**—Hillary Clinton, 2011**

# CONTENTS

# A COMPLICATED WOMAN

AS A YOUNG GIRL, SHE WAS A BOOKWORM, A teacher's pet, and a tomboy, too. Plenty of people claim a strong dislike for her and her ideas, but she has lots of good, loyal friends. She's warm and funny—also steely and disciplined. She's given to loud, merry laughter, but as a boss, she can be severe. She's cautious *and* brave. A generous woman of deep religious faith and a dedicated public servant, and yet she's not above getting angry and yelling at people. Her work is in the public spotlight, but she's famous for wanting her privacy. What are we to make of Hillary Rodham Clinton? Like most people, she's complicated.

Hillary came of age in the late 1960s and early 1970s. In that era of huge social changes, she met Bill Clinton, the future forty-second president. They fell in love, married, and formed one of the most important and controversial political partnerships in US history. She's been a First Lady, a vocal champion for the world's women and girls, a US senator, and her nation's sixty-seventh secretary of state. Now she's making her second run at the US presidency, the ultimate, historic *first* for women.

Ambitious, high-energy Hillary describes herself as "somebody who gets up every day and says, 'What am I going to do today, and how am I going to do it?'"

Her statement reflects her upbringing and iron-willed nature, but you can't fully know Hillary without knowing the words of John Wesley, the eighteenth-century founder of her Methodist faith: "Do all the good you can. By all the means you can. In all the ways you can. In all the places you can. At all the times you can. To all the people you can. As long as ever you can."

The lesson was tattooed on her heart when she was a Sunday-school girl in Illinois.

# CHAPTER 1
# BABY BOOMER

**October 26, 1947–June 9, 1965**
I was born an American in the middle of the
twentieth century, a fortunate time and place.
—Hillary Rodham Clinton, *Living History*

THE CONTINENTAL UNITED STATES DIDN'T SUFFER
the sort of battles and bombs that wrecked so much of
Europe and Asia in World War II. When it ended in 1945,
millions of US veterans came home to a powerful America. They were eager to see their families and start ones
of their own. The US birthrate was about to explode. Of
the nearly four million "baby boomers" born in 1947,
one was tiny Hillary Diane Rodham, first child of Hugh
and Dorothy Rodham of Chicago. Baby Hillary's sturdy,
pretty mother was born in Chicago too, on June 4, 1919,
but her young parents couldn't care for her. Little Dorothy
Howell was only eight when her mother put her and her

3

three-year-old sister on a train for a lonely, scary, four-day ride to California to live with their mean, strict grandmother. By the time she was fourteen, Dorothy was on her own, working as a cook, nanny, and housemaid. Luckily, her kind employers helped her finish high school, but college? Impossible. In time, Dorothy found secretarial work and a steady boyfriend, stocky, black-haired Hugh E. Rodham.

Hugh, a fabric salesman of Welsh ancestry, grew up in Scranton, Pennsylvania, and graduated from Pennsylvania State University. In early 1942, shortly after the United States entered World War II, Hugh and Dorothy were married. He joined the US Navy and served near Chicago, at Naval Station Great Lakes, training sailors for battle. After the war, Hugh started making and selling window shades and curtains. Dorothy helped with the business and had their daughter, on October 26, 1947. She named her Hillary, liking its exotic sound.

Events were happening in young Hillary's world that would shape her life and those of countless others. Black American soldiers, who had helped to win World War II, faced cruel race discrimination when they came home. Thousands of women who'd served in uniform or built tanks and bombers in US factories had to leave their jobs to make room for returning servicemen. Now they were expected to devote themselves to their homes, husbands, and children, as Hillary's mother did. And everyone lived in the Cold War's scary shadow.

## The Cold War

After its 1917 revolution, Russia and its neighbor countries became the Union of Soviet Socialist Republics, aka the USSR or Soviet Union. It was a communist (state owned and controlled) dictatorship. After World War II, the USSR seized control of Eastern Europe and isolated its citizens behind a virtual "Iron Curtain" between them and the democratic West, including the United States, which waged a long Cold War (a war of nerves rather than guns) to keep Soviet-style Communism from spreading. President Harry Truman went on TV (a White House first) in 1947 to say that the United States would help keep other countries from becoming part of the USSR's communist empire. The United States and the ever-more-powerful USSR competed in the arts and space exploration. They piled up bombs to fight each other, bombs that could destroy the world. Communism scared Americans so badly that they questioned their fellow citizens' patriotic loyalty and got into awful wars in Korea and Vietnam before the Cold War finally ended in 1991, when the Soviet Union crumbled.

Hugh Rodham did so well at his business and at saving money that he was able to buy a two-story brick house at 235 North Wisner Street, in Park Ridge, Illinois. Hillary's family moved into this well-to-do Chicago suburb in 1950, when she was three and her younger brother, Hugh Jr. (Hughie), was a baby. Their brother Tony came along in 1954. Hugh and Dorothy took their babies to Scranton to have each of them christened at Hugh's boyhood Methodist church. Not far away was a cabin that they visited every summer. Hillary and her little brothers swam in Lake Winola, played pinochle with their grandpa Rodham, and listened to his stories.

At home, four-year-old Hillary loved playing with all the neighborhood kids, but one day a tough little girl shoved her. If she was hit again, said Hillary's mom, she should hit the other girl back. "There's no room in this house for cowards," said Dorothy. She wanted her children to be confident and stand up for themselves. So Hillary minded her mother and came home in glory, puffed up with the other kids' respect, including that of the tough girl, Hillary's new friend. It was a strong and lasting lesson.

Hillary grew up riding her bike to Eugene Field Elementary and to the library. Like her mom, she loved books, card games, and board games. She earned good grades and Brownie badges, trying to please her much-loved dad. Alas, Hillary's strict, cantankerous father rarely praised anybody. He did show his daughter how to hit a baseball. Though she wasn't a natural athlete, she played hard, and sports taught her not to take defeat personally. Better luck next time. Besides, nobody beat Hillary at organizing a neighborhood game of kickball or a back-yard circus.

Dorothy taught her children to keep their emotions centered, like the bubble on a carpenter's level. Hugh taught them to root for the Chicago Cubs and not to expect allowances, even when they helped out at the family business. They must not waste *anything*. Leave a cap off the toothpaste and he'd toss it out the window for his children to find, even in the snow. No matter how cold the night, the furnace went off. Money was to be saved, not spent. And Republican Richard Nixon should have won the 1960 presidential election—definitely *not* John F. Kennedy, the Democrat.

Hillary agreed with her dad. She was a Republican too. Her mom's politics were more Democratic, but Dorothy kept that to herself around her forceful husband, in conservative Park Ridge.

After a Russian cosmonaut and then a US astronaut rocketed into space in 1961, young Hillary was inspired to write to NASA (National Aeronautics and Space Administration) to see how she could join the US space program. But Hillary was not destined to become an astronaut, and around this time an important mentor came into her life: the new youth minister at her church, the First United Methodist.

Reverend Don Jones wanted to open the minds of the white suburban teens in his flock. He introduced them to difficult books and fine art, and to the young people at Chicago's black and Hispanic churches. With Reverend Jones's encouragement, Hillary babysat for Mexican children whose families worked on the area farms. In spring 1962, Reverend Dr. Martin Luther King Jr. came to Chicago. Reverend Jones took Hillary and her friends to see, hear, and shake hands with the increasingly well-known civil rights activist. Hillary learned more about her country as well as the power of words well spoken. They could inspire people and move them to action.

## The Civil Rights Movement

After some three hundred years of buying, selling, and holding African Americans in forced servitude, legal slavery had become such a settled way of life in the American South that it took a four-year-long Civil War and a constitutional amendment to end the practice in 1865. Former slaves gained citizenship in 1868, but laws couldn't root out some whites' racist attitudes and cruel behavior. After years of deadly violence, the US government produced a parade of laws aimed at fairness and racial equality. In 1948 President Truman ordered the US armed forces to end segregation (separation by race). In 1954 the US Supreme Court ruled that public schools must be integrated (young people learning together). But American troops often had to protect brave black students from mobs of furious white people, who didn't want their world to change.

Behind every law, such as the Civil Rights Act of 1964 and the Voting Rights Act of 1965, were many marches, sit-ins at "whites-only" businesses, and countless acts of solitary courage. People faced getting fired, evicted, beaten, or jailed just for try-ing to vote. To integrate city buses in Montgomery, Alabama, in 1956, it took the leadership of activists like Dr. Martin Luther King Jr. and Rosa Parks. Black citizens boycotted (didn't ride) the buses for more than a year. All of this and more made up America's huge social change known as the civil rights movement.

When Hillary, high school dynamo, wasn't studying, she was busy with church and school activities like the student council, newspaper, National Honor Society, and girls' softball. As for dating, Hillary's protective father disapproved of most of the boys she liked and the dancing lessons she wanted. And he couldn't see why his daughter should have a driver's license when she had a perfectly good bicycle. At school, some kids thought she was stuck-up. She didn't always return their smiles—maybe because nearsighted Hillary couldn't see without her glasses. She'd worn them since she was in fourth grade, but Hillary thought she looked better when she took them *off*.

As a busy senior and a Republican, Hillary wrote a term paper about conservative (pro national defense, anti "big government" programs) Barry Goldwater. This Arizona senator was her choice in the 1964 presidential election. President John F. Kennedy would have been running again that year, if he hadn't been assassinated in Dallas, Texas. That was in November 1963, Hillary's junior year. So JFK's vice president, Lyndon B. Johnson, took office and became the Democrats' man in '64. Hillary's history teacher had introduced her to Senator Goldwater's writings. Alas, "Goldwater Girl" Hillary not only saw her candidate soundly defeated, she lost an election herself.

In her campaign for student government president, Hillary gave an impressive speech to the whole school, but she lost to a boy. She must be really stupid, a kid told her, to think that "a girl could be elected president." That stung. So Hillary did what she almost always did with her hurt feelings. She tamped them down and got busy running her school's organizations committee. She'd still have an important job—just one with less glory and a lot more work.

At last, on June 9, 1965, Hillary and the other "'65ers" prepared to don their red caps and gowns for the Maine Township High School South graduation. The Supremes, the Beach Boys, the Beatles, and the Four Tops played on their transistor radios—or, perhaps, news about America's ongoing war in Vietnam or black citizens' continuing battles at home for civil equality.

Hillary Rodham and millions of other baby boomers were leaving high school forever and stepping out into a tempestuous world. Who knew what lay ahead, for them and for their country?

## CHAPTER 2
# CHANGING TIMES

**Summer 1965–May 31, 1969**
The times they are a-changin'.
—Bob Dylan

We arrived not yet knowing what was not possible.
—Hillary Rodham

HILLARY CONSIDERED NEARBY COLLEGES, BUT WHEN two teachers she liked mentioned the northeastern schools they'd gone to, they sparked her interest. They'd attended two of the "Seven Sisters." Barnard, Vassar, Bryn Mawr, Radcliffe, Smith, Mount Holyoke, and Wellesley were women's colleges, founded in the 1800s, when most schools were men-only. Studious Hillary liked boys fine, but she didn't agree with how they seemed to be taken more seriously than girls or the way some girls down-played their intelligence when boys were around and did not speak up with their usual confidence.

For years, young ladies went to the "Sisters" to further their education, some hoping to find husbands at the men's colleges nearby. Hillary chose Wellesley, near Boston, because she liked the photographs of its rolling lakeside campus. In late summer 1965, her parents drove her there. Seeing that the students didn't look like some of the scruffy "beatniks" or "hippies" he'd read about, Hugh let Hillary stay, but then, after a few weeks, she didn't want to.

Miserable Hillary felt homesick, surrounded by smart, polished girls who'd had more advantages. Dorothy cried most of the way back to Illinois. She hated leaving her daughter, but she wasn't going to let her be a quitter and go through life as she had, afraid to do or say what she wanted.

Hillary cheered up as time passed and she got to know the other girls. They liked her warm combination of seriousness and fun. She liked the confident way girls spoke up in class and the casual way they dressed, with no guys around. Glasses? Not a problem. A girl could just swoop her hair back in a ponytail, a braid, or a messy bun, and anyone could be *somebody*. Hillary became president of Wellesley's Young Republicans Club. The members noted her natural leadership and how she expressed her well-researched, reasoned-out ideas. And Hillary met her first serious boyfriend. Until they parted on friendly terms, she and Harvard student Geoff Shields went together for three years.

Weekdays and nights were for classes, homework, and long talks about books, boyfriends, professors, music, politics, current events, and how things were done at Wellesley. For instance, how come their class of four hundred included only six African-American students? Wellesley's first black graduate, Harriet A. Rice, graduated in 1887. The times had changed since then, but not enough. In any case, Hillary became friends with Karen Williamson, Francille Wilson, and her other black classmates. She invited Karen to come to church with her one Sunday. How did friendship, political statement, and worship figure into her invitation? It's likely that Hillary herself couldn't have said.

Years later, Hillary recalled her classmates saying, "Wellesley was a girls' school when we started and a women's college when we left." In Hillary's first years, girls complained about Wellesley's old-fashioned rules and traditions, like having to put on a skirt or dress before going to the dining hall. It was as if their parents were there, checking their watches on weeknights, making sure girls were in their dorms by eleven p.m. When they went to weekend "mixers" to dance with college guys, they had to be in by one a.m. Were they allowed to have male "callers" in their dorm rooms? Certainly not, except for Sundays between two and five thirty p.m., if the door was left open and two of a couple's four feet were on the floor at all times.

But the sixties were years of great social change. Sweaters and pleated skirts gave way to peasant blouses, jeans, and embroidered bell-bottoms. The Wellesley girls changed. Hillary's politics changed, and America did too.

## The Women's Liberation Movement

Betty Friedan's 1963 bombshell of a bestseller, *The Feminine Mystique*, touched off the second wave of a long fight for women's full equality. The first was their 1848–1920 fight for the right to vote. Mrs. Friedan, a journalist and a mom, devoted much thought and research to her idea: Women loved their families, but so many of them felt isolated and unhappy as homemakers, their society-approved career path. Invisible barriers kept them out of "male" professions such as engineering, politics, television broadcasting, and law.

As women talked about Friedan's book and their

own unequal opportunities, paychecks, promotions, and relationships, a movement formed. Soon the women's movement became a social revolution. Betty Friedan and other determined feminists founded the National Organization for Women in 1966. The Equal Rights Amendment (ERA) got fresh attention too. Women had first presented the ERA to Congress in 1923, hoping to have their rights guaranteed by the US Constitution. (The amendment has never been voted into proper law.)

Revolutionary too was what happened in 1960. The federal government approved a drug that gave women control over whether or not they would have babies. By 1967, 12.5 million women worldwide were on "the Pill."

The women's movement ripples through our society to this day. Title IX of 1972's Education Amendments opened up federally funded sports and other activities to girls. Women's liberation paved the way for Shirley Chisholm, the first black woman to run for president, in 1972, for a major political party. And Geraldine Ferraro achieved another first for women when, in 1984, the Democrats chose her to be their vice presidential candidate.

Even more than the civil rights and women's movements, nothing affected young Hillary's thinking like the Vietnam War. When she was a fifth grader, in the Cold War years,

US leaders got tangled in Vietnam's troubles in order to get Communism out of Southeast Asia. So many citizens disagreed over their government's actions in Vietnam that a deep political divide began to split the American people.

## The Vietnam War

For about a thousand years, the ancient Vietnamese had to tolerate Chinese invaders. Later on, in the late 1800s, Vietnam, plus Laos and Cambodia, became the French colony Indochina. Japan ruled it in World War II. Afterward, France wanted its control back, but Ho Chi Minh and other Vietnamese nationalists fought the better equipped, American-funded French forces until they finally surrendered. This **First Indochina War** ended in 1954 with a divided Vietnam.

Victorious Ho Chi Minh controlled North Vietnam, and very harshly too. Because he was a Communist, the USSR helped him. So did Red China, called that because (1) the USSR's flag was red, and (2) China went communist in 1949.

To keep Communism from spreading further, the United States sent money plus hundreds of advisers to South Vietnam. But the US-backed leader ruled so poorly that thousands of South Vietnamese fought his government. These were the Viet Cong. Ho Chi Minh sent fighters too. The **Second Indochina War** had begun. Americans know it as the **Vietnam War**.

Before President Kennedy died in 1963, he sent thousands more military advisers to Southeast Asia.

After a 1964 clash, President Johnson got Congress's permission to fight North Vietnam, but with no proper declaration of war, as in World War II. In 1965 about sixty thousand US troops were in Vietnam. By 1968, there were more than 543,000. Americans hated seeing weary, wounded soldiers on the nightly TV news. The war was costing billions of dollars, when money might be better spent on helping Americans at home.

American troops stayed in Vietnam until 1975. More than 58,000 died, besides some 300,000 wounded and many thousands of veterans psychologically damaged by the war experience. More than a million Vietnamese soldiers and countless civilians were killed. In 1976, seven years after Ho Chi Minh died at age seventy-nine, Vietnam became a unified Communist nation.

For the young people of Hillary's generation, a most upsetting part of the Vietnam War era was the draft. Unless they were full-time students or they could prove that they were against the war for religious reasons, men could be drafted (forced by law) into military service. Many patriotic young men wondered if they would or even should serve, if they seriously disagreed with their nation's war. It was a difficult legal and moral question at a very troubling time. Some looked for important people to help them dodge (avoid) the draft. Others went into hiding or left the country, often for Canada. Some burned their draft cards (official registration cards from the US Selective Service) in public acts of protest. More than 265,000 female volunteers served in Vietnam, but this was a time when young women earnestly considered the question: If they could be drafted, what would they do?

Hillary was raised to be a "hawk," someone who believed that the United States had to crush Communism wherever it was. But as she studied the Vietnam War, demonstrations by pro-peace "doves" began making more sense to her. Hillary began rethinking her basic outlook. It was as if her heart could no longer agree with her conservative mind. During her sophomore year, in February 1967, Hillary's inner argument turned into a deep sadness. Who was she, really? What should she do with her life?

She wanted to help people, but how exactly—as a professor or as a political leader? After all, as a political science major, Hillary was learning about the ways and methods of politics and governments. What if she became an activist, who gave speeches and organized campaigns for peace and social justice? The more Hillary wondered where she should direct her energies, the less energy she seemed to have. Finally, she willed herself up and out of her depression and got busy. She threw herself back into her studies, leading discussions and organizing efforts to improve the world around her. She showed such skill at these activities that she was chosen to head an elite group of juniors, who advised beginning freshmen. And she chose to run for the presidency of Wellesley's student government.

Hillary went from dorm to dorm, door to door, finding out what students wanted. Then she spoke up for a pass-fail grading system, more campus diversity, and definitely more freedom. This time, in February 1968, Hillary won. It was just the beginning of a political season like none other.

Hillary, former president of Wellesley's Young Republicans, volunteered to help Democratic Minnesota senator Eugene McCarthy's presidential campaign. Both he and New York senator Bobby Kennedy (brother of the assassinated president) wanted to win the presidency away from President Lyndon B. Johnson. Both men were against the Vietnam War, which LBJ couldn't seem to win, yet could not bear to lose. Still, few expected powerful President Johnson to drop out of the race, but he did, in a televised message to the nation, March 31, 1968.

Only one man expected what happened four days later: the assassin who murdered Dr. Martin Luther King Jr. in Memphis, Tennessee.

"I can't take it," a tearful Hillary shouted when she heard the horrifying news. She'd met Dr. King and admired him and his work. When grieving protesters marched in Boston on April 5, Hillary marched with them.

In reaction to Dr. King's death, a fiery wave of violence swept through US cities. Their own fury and sorrow gave Karen Williamson and Wellesley's other black students the courage to *demand* change. As their friend and head of the student government, Hillary added her voice, demanding increased black enrollment, funding for scholarships, a black studies class, and a tutoring program for inner-city children, all of which came to pass.

Just weeks after Dr. King's murder, Hillary was home for summer vacation. Her mother woke her with still more horrible news: someone in Los Angeles had shot Bobby Kennedy. He died on June 6, 1968. Hillary and millions of other despairing Americans wondered what on earth was happening in their country.

Hillary did her best to pull herself together. She had a trip to take and a job to do. She'd won a place in Welles-

ley's internship program. For nine weeks she worked in
Washington, DC, in the office of Republican representative Melvin Laird. He posed for a picture with her and
two other Republican congressmen, Charles Goodell and
Gerald R. Ford, the future president. (Hugh Rodham
framed the photo and proudly hung it on his wall.) Then
the interns got to visit the Republican convention in
Miami Beach. Hillary relished the chance to see history in
the making as well as work behind the scenes in big-time
politics and have her first stay in a fancy hotel.

She hoped that moderate New York governor Rocke-
feller would be nominated, but the party chose conservative Richard Nixon. This was so upsetting that Hillary
gave up on the Republicans once and for all and went
home to Park Ridge. But the dramatic, historic political
season wasn't done yet. Hillary and her high school buddy,
Betsy Johnson, told their parents they were off to the movies in Chicago—where the Democrats were holding their
national convention, their intended destination all along.

As Hillary and Betsy neared the location, they smelled
the tear gas swirling through the steamy summer night,
stinging their eyes. They heard and saw helmeted officers
and war protesters screaming and cursing at one another.

They saw men swinging their clubs. They saw blood-ied faces. Americans' angry feelings about Vietnam, the deaths of King and Kennedy, racial violence raging—all were reflected in the Democrats' stormy convention. In the end, they nominated Vice President Hubert H. Humphrey, who lost to Mr. Nixon in the fall of Hillary's senior year at Wellesley.

She plunged into studying for her classes and researching her final thesis. Hillary decided to write about Chicago's author/activist Saul Alinsky. She admired how he showed poor people, on the bottom rungs of society's ladder, ways of organizing their actions to force social change. She saw how powerful people could be when they worked together. Still, in her heart, Hillary believed that government offered the best operating system for improving society. In fact, she decided to become a lawyer, all the better to work in that system.

Hillary and millions of other baby boomers were graduating from college in 1969, a historical milestone. As it happened, Wellesley's students and other young tradition busters wanted one of their own to speak at their commencement—a radical innovation. Hillary's classmates chose her. Her photo appeared in *Life*, the megapopular national magazine, along with her words and those of four other student speakers.

Sadly, Dorothy Rodham had medical problems that kept her from going with Hugh to see their daughter graduate on May 31, 1969. After the official speaker finished his remarks, Wellesley's president introduced "cheerful, good humored" Hillary. She stepped to the microphone, glasses on, nervousness tamped down, her long, dark blond hair swept up in a bun.

"We're not in the positions yet of leadership and power," she said, "but we do have that indispensable task of criticizing and constructive protest." Then Hillary reported on the progress that had resulted from her class's efforts "to forge an identity in this particular age." After all, the goal of education must be "human liberation," a life lived with "integrity, the courage to be whole . . . living in relation to one another in the full poetry of existence," with mutual respect and trust. She concluded with a poem by her classmate Nancy Scheibner. Its ending spoke of practicing "with all the skill of our being the art of making possible."

The poem's final words were well suited to the day.

Hillary was rewarded with a standing ovation. More than one of her classmates was sure she had the makings of America's first woman president. With her new bachelor of arts degree in political science, her intelligence, ambition, and all the skills of her being, twenty-one-year-old Hillary Rodham was determined to take on the world and make it better.

CHAPTER 3

# LAW. LIFE. LOVE.

**Autumn 1969–Spring 1973**
You have to be true to yourself.
—Hillary Rodham Clinton

AFTER FOUR DIFFICULT YEARS OF STUDYING, HILLARY was eager to rest her brain. She hit the road to Alaska. After a summer of washing dishes at Mount McKinley (now Denali) National Park and cleaning salmon at Valdez, she was ready to head back to school.

When she entered law school in the fall of 1969, Hillary was a genuine rarity. Women were only 5 percent of the US legal profession then. Today they make up about a third. A snooty Harvard professor had told Hillary that Harvard Law School had enough women, thank you. So she went to Yale, in New Haven, Connecticut, to join the twenty-six other female and 208 male first-year law students, as a cultural storm rumbled over America.

The Vietnam War still raged and sparked arguments among American citizens. Many of the soldiers there had been drafted. They might have avoided the draft if they'd had the means to go to college. Among these fighting men were African Americans, who'd faced continuing discrimination at home and when they'd served their country overseas. So, besides loud demands for equal rights and to stop the war, Hillary's stormy country rang with cries of "Black Power."

## Black Power

In the early 1900s, Marcus Garvey said that Africans around the world should unite. They should be proud of their race and their culture and not let white people determine who had beauty and worth. In the 1960s, activist Stokely Carmichael morphed the message into "Black is beautiful." And he'd thunder, "Black Power!" Fearing African-American violence, law enforcement agents watched him, Dr. King, and other black leaders. As for Huey P. Newton and Bobby Seale, they came to believe that nonviolence was too slow a path to full equality, if it was even possible in a racist America. So they formed the **Black Panther Party**. Unfortunately, more than once, in the Panthers' violent efforts to end black citizens' unfair treatment, there was gunfire.

Hillary was still at Wellesley when a young man in New Haven was killed. His fellow Black Panthers thought he'd been giving inside info to the FBI (Federal Bureau of Investigation) and were accused of the murder. In April 1970, when nine Panthers went on trial, Hillary and some of her fellow law students were assigned to attend the trial, to make sure that it was conducted properly.

Fearful that the Panthers would not be treated fairly, thousands of their supporters came to New Haven. The town and Yale's campus were already alive with hippie vagabonds, eager to protest the Vietnam War at the big peace demonstration scheduled for May 1. The spring air was full of talk and music: Jimi Hendrix, Janis Joplin, and the Rolling Stones. It all drifted around banners, tents, and buses painted with symbols of peace, raised fists, and mind-bending psychedelic designs. This was the scene when, late on April 27, someone set fire to Yale's law library. Hillary ran to help on the bucket brigade and save the books. When students and university administrators met the next day to argue and despair over the fire, Hillary did her level-headed best to make sure everyone was heard.

To compound the already heated domestic troubles, President Nixon went on TV on April 30 to say he was sending US troops into Cambodia to stop the North Vietnamese from moving soldiers and supplies to South Vietnam along Cambodian trails. He thought this would shorten the war. Millions of Americans thought he was just expanding it. At Ohio's Kent State University, angry students torched the ROTC (Reserve Officer Training Corps) building. On May 4, after US National Guardsmen fired into a crowd of the protesters there, nine fell wounded. Four lay dead. Afterward, thousands of furious students all over the country went on strike. Hundreds of colleges closed down. Hillary was still mourning "the Kent State Four" when her life turned an important corner.

Not long after Hillary spoke at a Washington, DC, banquet honoring fifty years since American women won the right to vote and founded the League of Women Voters, she met Marian Wright Edelman. Ms. Edelman, an African-American lawyer Hillary very much admired, had founded the Washington Research Project, an agency to check on federal programs for low-income families. In her, Hillary found an important mentor *and* a summer job.

As a fieldworker for the WRP, she gathered information for US senators investigating the well-being of migrant farmworkers' children and the discrimination they faced in the public schools. As a girl in Illinois, Hillary had looked after farmworkers' children. She still remembered seven-year-old Maria, whose parents couldn't afford the dress she needed for her First Communion. Hillary had told her mother, who knew all about little girls not having what they needed. Dorothy and her daughter went out and bought the prettiest white dress they could find, and Hillary never forgot Maria's mother's happy tears.

In her fieldwork, in her work at Yale's Child Study Center, New Haven's hospital, and a legal services office, Hillary saw the troubles some kids had. She decided to focus on defending children's rights in court, a new area in the legal profession. Kids who'd been abused or neglected, as her mom had been, needed someone to speak for them. All this was on Hillary's mind in the autumn she turned twenty-three, when she noticed a new student at Yale Law School. It was difficult not to.

Hillary thought twenty-four-year-old Bill Clinton looked "like a Viking." He was tall: six foot two to her five seven, with a "reddish-brown beard and curly mane of hair." He was bragging about the giant watermelons back home in Arkansas. Few would have suspected that this country fellow had spent the last two years studying government at England's Oxford University, thanks to a Rhodes scholarship awarded only to outstanding students with a knack for leadership.

Soon enough, Bill noticed outspoken Hillary, the serious girl with the long, thick, dark blond hair. They kept noticing each other but didn't get acquainted until she introduced herself in the spring of 1971.

They fell into a conversation that continued as they walked across Yale's leafy campus. With his vast reading and terrific memory, Bill could talk about almost any subject, especially government, its ways and uses. As for Bill, he'd never met anyone so intensely smart, spiritual, and idealistic as confident, direct Hillary Rodham. "She was in my face from the start," he'd say later on, "and, before I knew it, in my heart."

"He was the first man I'd met," Hillary would remember, "who wasn't afraid of me." She could relate to Bill's ambition and passion for politics (both squarely aimed at becoming the governor of Arkansas), but she loved the way Bill showed up with orange juice and chicken soup the minute he heard that she was sick with a cold.

Each felt lucky and amazed to have attracted the other's interest and affection.

In 1971 candidates were gearing up for the '72 election. Hillary lined up a summer job in an Oakland, California, law office. Bill had a job with Senator George McGovern's presidential campaign. (The South Dakota Democrat was for ending the Vietnam War.) But political Bill stunned Hillary, saying he'd rather be with her. Why would he give up doing something he loved so much to follow her to California?

"For someone I love," Bill replied, "that's why."

Having completed Yale Law School's three-year program in 1972, Hillary could have left New Haven. Instead, she stayed to work and to be with Bill, who'd begun his law studies a year after she had. They scoured secondhand shops to furnish their drafty little home together. While Bill studied and worked in the McGovern for President office he'd set up, Hillary helped two of her professors research their book on child development. She wrote her first scholarly article, "Children Under the Law." She and Bill read, took yoga classes, held hands at the movies, and planned Bill's Christmas visit to Park Ridge.

He wasn't the first beau Hillary had brought home to meet her dour, conservative father. Hugh Rodham had never liked his daughter's boyfriends. Now here was Bill Clinton, a long-haired Democrat with sideburns. But Bill specialized in being friendly. He won Hugh over, talking sports, playing cards, and watching football with him and Hillary's brothers. He talked with Dorothy about the college class she was taking. And once Hillary's friends saw how Bill made her laugh, they told her not to let him get away. It wasn't likely. Hillary was in love.

It was 1972. President Richard Nixon was determined to win a second term. But events were taking place that would affect the election, Hillary's career, and the nation's history.

## The Watergate Scandal

Late on June 17, 1972, in Washington, DC, five men got caught breaking into the Democratic Party's office in the Watergate complex. Two *Washington Post* reporters, Carl Bernstein and Bob Woodward, discovered that those burglars were there to plant "bugs" so their bosses could listen in on the Democrats' plans. Moreover, they were part of a scheme to make sure President Nixon defeated Senator McGovern in 1972. He did, but not without spies and skullduggery.

Nixon said he didn't know about the mischief, but in May 1973, the attorney general (AG, head of the Justice Department) chose a special prosecutor, an official lawyer, to look into the matter. So did US senators, on TV, for all the citizens to see. The president's ex-lawyer John Dean said that Nixon *did* know what was going on. There was proof: Nixon recorded all his Oval Office conversations. But he wouldn't let anyone listen to the tapes, not even an important judge. When the prosecutor said that he must, Nixon ordered the AG to fire him. The AG refused, then resigned; the deputy AG quit too. Only when President Nixon faced serious charges of official misconduct did he release his recordings—minus minutes mysteriously erased.

It was a tremendous, historic political scandal. Members of the president's staff were arrested. Vice President Spiro Agnew resigned. Representative Gerald Ford became the new vice president, and the president himself faced impeachment.

For a time, in the summer of 1972, Hillary worked for Ms. Edelman, checking on private schools set up by white Southerners, separate from the racially integrated public schools. Then Hillary joined Bill in Texas, to work for Senator McGovern. She drummed up Democratic voters in the black and Hispanic communities, especially young people, now that the Twenty-Sixth Amendment had lowered the US voting age from twenty-one to eighteen.

Among Hillary and Bill's new Texas friends were two more seasoned political experts. Betsey Wright and Sara Ehrman were especially impressed with smart, goal-driven Hillary. In their opinion, her political future could be far brighter than her boyfriend's. Years later Ms. Ehrman remembered, "She was so smart and focused and organized."

Bill Clinton was impressed with her too, but he had another future in mind for Hillary Rodham. After she and Bill graduated from Yale Law School in 1973, he took Hillary to England. There, beside a crystal-blue lake, he asked her to marry him.

## CHAPTER 4

# ARKANSAS BALANCING ACT

**August 1974–October 3, 1991**
I knew I was always happier with Bill than without him.
—Hillary Rodham Clinton

## "NO," SAID HILLARY, "NOT NOW."

Bill proposed again and still, she said no. Hillary loved him, but wasn't ready to commit to dynamic Bill Clinton.

He was prepared to wait. Bill wanted her to be sure. Meanwhile, he taught law classes at the University of Arkansas (UA) in Fayetteville, in the state's hilly northwest. Hillary went to Cambridge, Massachusetts, to work with Ms. Edelman's new Children's Defense Fund (CDF). She counted children in New Bedford, Massachusetts, who were attending school. Some wanted to but couldn't because of their disabilities. Hillary's study helped the CDF convince Congress to pass the 1975 Education for

All Handicapped Children Act. In South Carolina, Hillary investigated jailed teenagers' living conditions. Her findings there helped the CDF's efforts to get teens housed away from grown-up offenders. Then Hillary went to investigate life in Arkansas with Bill. She missed him.

He met Hillary's flight and took her to see his favorite places around the capital city of Little Rock. Bill drove past the governor's mansion—their future home, if he had his way. Then he took Hillary to Hot Springs, his storied hometown.

For centuries, people had come there to bathe in the natural mineral springs. From the late 1800s until the 1960s, when the illegal gambling was shut down, Hot Springs was a playground for famous mobsters such as Al Capone. Big stars performed at the hotels when they weren't at the casinos, bathhouses, and racetracks with regular people like Bill's vivacious mother. She'd lived there for years with Bill's stepfather and half brother, Roger Clinton Jr. Early in Hillary's relationship with Bill Clinton, the name he took at age fourteen, she learned what a challenging youth he had experienced.

## William Jefferson Clinton

Bill started out as William Jefferson Blythe III, son of Virginia Cassidy, twenty-three, and Bill Blythe

Jr., twenty-eight, killed in a car wreck on May 17, 1946, three months before Bill was born. Baby Billy was born August 19, 1946, in tiny Hope, Arkansas. Virginia was a registered nurse, but to better support herself and her son, she left him with her parents and went to Louisiana. There she studied to add administering anesthesia to her nursing skills. Smart, chubby Billy loved hanging around Grandpa Cassidy's store, listening to the black and white customers' conversations, and looking at the books he was learning to read.

Back in Hope, in 1950, Virginia married Roger Clinton. Then, in 1953, they moved with six-year-old Billy to Hot Springs, where Roger had a job at his big brother's car dealership. In time, he became a violent alcoholic, a threat to Virginia as well as Bill and little Roger Jr. When he was big enough, fifteen-year-old Bill ordered his stepfather to quit harming his mother and talked her into divorcing Roger, but Virginia soon remarried him.

Like his mother, Bill hid his troubles behind a sunny smile. He earned top grades, played saxophone in his high school band, and loved the Baptists' hymn singing on Sundays. At Boys State, an American Legion civics program, he found his passion for politics and government. It led him to Boys Nation in Washington, DC, in July 1963, where he shook hands with his hero, thirty-fifth president, John F. Kennedy. By the time Bill graduated from Georgetown University, his stepfather was dead, but Virginia lived to see her son in the White House.

When Bill introduced Hillary to his mother, the two women he loved best were shocked at the sight of each other. As a serious young feminist of her times, long-haired Hillary avoided frivolous makeup, dresses, and high heels. She wore jeans. Bill's flashy mother had drawn-on eyebrows, false eyelashes, frosted eye shadow, and bright red lips. Her black-dyed bouffant hairdo was streaked with a frosty white stripe. But Virginia had this in common with Hillary: they both loved Bill Clinton.

In 1974, Bill, twenty-seven, was in the midst of his first big campaign, and he was aiming high: a seat in the US House of Representatives, where the Watergate scandal was *the* hot topic of discussion—and soon, the focus of an official investigation. Extra lawyers were going to be needed. So it was that twenty-six-year-old Hillary Rodham was hired to help prepare charges against the president of the United States.

## Impeachment

Only the House of Representatives can impeach (bring charges against) the president, vice president, or other high government officials. If a majority of the representatives votes for impeachment, the Senate becomes a court. The Supreme Court's chief justice presides as judge. If two-thirds of the senators vote against the impeached official, he or she is convicted.

Andrew Johnson had been the one and only president to have been impeached, in 1868. He wasn't convicted of the charges brought by his political enemies. He served until his term ended, March 4, 1869.

In Washington, DC, Hillary moved in with her Texas friend, Sara Ehrman. Then, suddenly, after seven months of intense work, the legal proceedings ended. Rather than face impeachment, disgraced President Nixon resigned his office on August 9, 1974. Hillary, too, was now unemployed. What would she do? Return to the Children's Defense Fund? Climb her career ladder even higher in Washington? Or would she follow her heart and let all her friends believe she was crazy?

Hillary thought of the important work that she and Bill could do together, with their love of government and for each other. She was certain that with her skills, their smarts, and his political genius, Bill Clinton could be president. Besides, she was so happy when she was with him. So she talked Sara into driving with her and her belongings to Arkansas.

Ms. Ehrman was of Hillary's mother's generation. She

and others had worked for years to win respect for women in the halls of power. More than once on the long drive to Fayetteville, Sara asked Hillary if she was sure about what she was doing.

"No," Hillary kept saying, "but I'm going anyway."

Like Bill, Hillary taught law at the University of Arkansas. She established UA's legal aid clinic too, where her students learned how to help their underprivileged clients. Hillary went to barbecues and football games with Bill and their friends. She shared lunchtimes and tennis games with her new best lifelong friend, Diane Kincaid. Ms. Kincaid was a historian and political science lecturer at UA and another easterner whose serious relationship had drawn her to Arkansas. There were other people in this small college town, though, who didn't know what to make of Hillary Rodham, with her liberal ideas, baggy clothes, and pushy, Yankee way of talking—and the way she meddled in Bill's political campaign.

Bill taught classes to pay the rent. What he *loved* was politicking: meeting voters, shaking their hands, and talking about what he'd do for them as their Democrat in the Congress. Hillary gave Bill lots of advice. She and her brother Tony and even her dad worked to help him win his election. But she was against taking money from people who'd only want favors later, in return for their donations. To Bill's campaign staffers, his idealistic northern girlfriend had no business interfering.

As it happened, Bill lost his first election. Hillary decided to go back to the Northeast for a while, for time with her family, friends, and serious thinking about her and Bill's future. As Bill drove her to the airport, Hillary complimented a little house they passed. As for Bill, he loved Hillary's passionate seriousness and how hard she worked for him. But he didn't like keeping her from her own brilliant career in the important cities back East. Still, while Hillary was away, he bought that small brick house she liked and told her so when she decided to return. "So now you'd better marry me," said Bill, "because I can't live in it by myself."

Hearing the news of the house *and* their daughter's upcoming wedding, Hugh, Dorothy, and Hillary's brothers traveled down to Fayetteville. Hillary went to the mall with her mom and grabbed an ivory lacy dress off the rack. She even put her hair in curlers for the next day,

October 11, 1975, when she married Bill Clinton in the parlor of their little brick house. Then she made her new mother-in-law cry—modern Hillary Rodham refused to give up her own independent identity by being known as "Mrs. Bill Clinton." And why should she and her new husband go off on some traditional honeymoon? As soon as the newlyweds taught their remaining law classes, they took off on their wedding trip to Acapulco, Mexico, along with all of the bride's family.

Afterward, Bill started his second campaign, traveling all over Arkansas to be his state's next attorney general. In July 1976, the Bicentennial election year, he and Hillary flew to New York City for the Democrats' convention to nominate a presidential candidate, Georgia governor Jimmy Carter. Hillary got a job managing his Indiana campaign while Bill worked for Carter in Arkansas and on his own race to be state attorney general.

In November 1976, Governor Carter lost Indiana, but he won Arkansas *and* the presidency. Bill Clinton celebrated his own political victory, his first. For the next two years, he'd work in Arkansas's capital city of Little Rock, but what would Hillary do there?

In her work at the Fayetteville legal clinic, Hillary had

worked with Vincent Foster, one of the partners at the Rose Law Firm (officially Rose, Nash, Williamson, Carroll, Clay, and Giroir). Bill had known Vince since they were young boys in Hope. Hillary wanted to work at the distinguished law firm. But in all its 156-year history, the Rose firm had *never* hired a female lawyer, much less a social reformer married to the state's AG. But Vince Foster and Webster "Webb" Hubbell, one of the other partners, argued for experienced Hillary Rodham. She, in turn, spoke very well for herself and got the job.

As attorney general, Bill focused on keeping officials and dairymen, respectively, from raising the prices of ten-cent pay-phone calls and milk. Every so often, he and Hillary were invited to the White House for dinner with the president and First Lady Rosalynn Carter. President Carter offered Hillary an extra part-time position, helping to direct the nation's Legal Services Corporation. This federal agency connected low-income Americans with free legal help.

At the Rose firm, Hillary learned about corporate law. However, learning to *look* the part proved to be a bit of a struggle. She didn't look anything like the other well-dressed and made-up women at the firm—secretaries, clerks, and such. Hillary's new good friends Vince and Webb laughed as she told them about the female clients who offered to give her makeovers. She tried to be more stylish and corporate, but lawyerly challenges interested Ms. Rodham far more than fashion.

Hillary lost her first solo case. She had to defend a cannery from a customer's lawsuit. (The man found a rat's tail section in a can of pork and beans.) For Hillary, even worse than losing, and then having to hear all the rat bottom jokes, was how nervous she was talking in court. She didn't give up, but Hillary preferred working behind the scenes at the firm, in the Legal Services board meetings, and in the work closest to her heart, for families and children. In one of her pro bono ("for good," no charge) cases, she helped a couple adopt their foster child. She helped start Arkansas's nonprofit Advocates for Children and Families, to provide resources and information for making fairer child-welfare laws. Additionally, busy Hillary had another concern. Like her dad, she believed in saving up a "nest egg" for her family's future.

Wanting her savings to grow quickly, she met with her and Bill's friend Jim Blair, a wealthy lawyer who traded in the risky futures business. With Blair's encouragement, Hillary invested $1,000 on cattle futures and made $100,000. But eventually she stepped away. Such trading was nerve-racking. She and Bill looked for a steadier investment, like real estate.

Bill's banker friend Jim McDougal had a deal in mind. In 1978, together with Jim and his wife Susan, Hillary and Bill borrowed money to buy a 230-acre piece of land up by Arkansas's White River. They formed a little company, the Whitewater Development Corporation, for the business of selling lots for vacation homes there. At the time, it seemed like a solid idea.

While Hillary poured her tremendous energies into her busy days, Bill campaigned in 1978 to become Arkansas's governor, the job he'd always wanted. His political enemies said lots of negative things about his nontraditional wife, but Bill Clinton won more than 60 percent of the vote. At last, in January 1979, he and Hillary would move into that governor's mansion he'd shown her the day she came to be with him. A little over a year later, Governor Clinton and the First Lady of Arkansas became parents.

Once Bill promised the doctors he wouldn't throw up or faint, they allowed him to don a pair of scrubs and hold

Hillary's hand. Chelsea Victoria Clinton was born just before midnight on February 27, 1980. Her name came from a song by singer/songwriter Joni Mitchell that her parents loved, "Chelsea Morning."

When her baby was four months old, Hillary Rodham went back to work. This upset many Arkansans, who wanted their governor's wife to behave like a "traditional" mom, one who didn't leave her baby in the care of taxpayer-paid staff people. Why couldn't she stay in the mansion, plan dinner parties, *and* use her husband's last name?

The criticism hurt Hillary's feelings. Why could people not see she was a careerwoman who was committed to her family? Still, she wrote later on, "I learned the hard way that some voters in Arkansas were seriously offended by the fact that I kept my maiden name."

## Governor of Arkansas, Part I:
### Jan. 9, 1979–Jan. 19, 1981

At thirty-two, Bill was Arkansas's youngest governor ever, and he was eager to put all his ideas to work, improving his relatively poor state. He secured federal funds for rural health clinics. But young Governor Clinton upset the timber industry by criticizing the way loggers left swaths of forest bare, endangering the state's rivers. Because heavy trucks wore out the roads, he proposed raising taxes on them and limiting their weight, which angered the trucking industry and the powerful poultry farmers, who shipped chickens in those big rigs. Then, to get funds to fix his state's 8,154 miles of highways, Bill angered Arkansans by increasing the fees for their motor vehicle licenses. And now, in 1980, just as voters nationwide were troubled by the poor economy and the fact that fifty-two Americans had been imprisoned by revolutionaries in Iran since November 1979 (and would be until January 1981), Bill faced reelection—and an international crisis.

Earlier in 1980, some 125,000 Cubans had escaped to America. President Carter sent 19,000 of them to Fort Chaffee, Arkansas, where they faced a slow screening process before they could settle in the United States. They grew so frustrated that some rioted, staged hunger strikes, or tried to escape. This situation, along with his other political troubles, cost Bill the election. Both Governor Clinton and President Carter lost to Republicans (Frank White and Ronald Reagan) that year.

When Bill failed to be reelected in 1980, he and Hillary were devastated. Bill felt as if he had failed at the job he was born to do. The mistakes he'd made kept parading through his memory. During this time, Chelsea's parents found their chief happiness in reading to her and playing with her. When Bill wasn't at his law office job, he cradled and sang to Chelsea. Hillary's spirits were revived too, by the talks she gave about her strong Methodist faith. She argued and coaxed Bill back to his optimism and his love for politics.

Bill announced his second run for governor on February 27, 1982, the day Chelsea turned two. Beside him stood his stylish wife, Hillary Rodham *Clinton*. She'd worked long and hard to establish her own professional identity, but to help Bill win his election, she took his last name for her own.

Bill and Hillary hired a consultant to help them find out Arkansans' main concerns. They hired political strategist Betsey Wright to get Bill and his office organized and into campaign mode. Armed with information, firm intentions, and a toys-and-snacks bag for Chelsea, the Clintons traveled Arkansas. They met voters, apologized for past mistakes, and promised a better future. Hillary even tracked down Governor Frank White, out campaigning for his reelection. When he spoke negatively about Bill, Hillary spoke up and talked back. And on Election Day 1982, White lost to Bill Clinton, 45 to 55 percent.

## Governor of Arkansas, Part II:
### Jan. 11, 1983–Dec. 12, 1992

Governor Clinton appointed Hillary to lead his Education Standards Committee. They were determined to improve Arkansas's schools. Hillary traveled the state, studying every district's curriculum, listening to citizens, and she took her findings to the legislature. Bill raised the sales tax and arranged budget money so all Arkansas's schools could provide kindergarten, more science and math classes, programs for gifted and talented students, and raises for low-paid teachers. But rather than just giving the schools money, the governor proposed student testing—and a basic skills test for the teachers. This infuriated their union, but Bill was reelected to a second two-year term in 1984. A rising tide of positive national attention lifted him to top positions in the National Governors Association and the Democratic Leadership Council. After the governor's term of office was extended to four years, Bill was reelected in 1986 and to a fifth term in 1990. Bill said he would serve all four years, but it was a promise he wouldn't—or couldn't—keep. The White House beckoned.

Returning to the Arkansas governor's mansion in 1983, Hillary stayed busy, with Chelsea, Chelsea's homework and ballet lessons, her own First Lady duties, her job at the Rose Law Firm, and service on various boards of directors. She had a voice in the running of Arkansas-based Walmart, as its first female director. Did she support the employees when they tried to form a union? No, but she did push this giant Arkansas business to hire more women and get "greener" with their recycling. All of Hillary's work earned her a place on the *National Law Journal*'s list of "The 100 Most Influential Lawyers in America" twice. She was named Arkansas's Woman of the Year in 1983, and its Young Mother of the Year in 1984. As to Hillary's roles as daughter and wife, the late 1980s brought her fresh challenges.

After Hillary's father had a stroke, the Clintons helped Hugh and Dorothy Rodham move to Little Rock to better look after them. This extra responsibility contributed to a painful chapter in Hillary's life. Bill wanted to run for president in 1988, but he and Hillary decided that the harsh attention that went with a demanding national campaign would be too hard on eight-year-old Chelsea and on their personal lives as well. So 1988 was Michael Dukakis's year to run against Ronald Reagan's vice president, George H. W. Bush.

Still, the Democrats invited Governor Clinton to speak at their convention. It was Bill's chance to shine on a national stage. Alas, with all he was told to say, Bill talked so long that the crowd booed. He was joke material for comics. But "bounce-back" Bill saved his talkative reputation by making fun of himself on national television, on Johnny Carson's *Tonight Show*.

As it happened, Mike Dukakis lost that election. During his four years as president, George H. W. Bush oversaw the USSR's collapse and the end of the Cold War. And, in distant Iraq, he waged Operation Desert Storm.

Meanwhile, Bill fell into one of his rare but deep bouts of gloom, which left him wondering if he wanted to stay in politics. So, in 1990, Hillary figured that if Bill hadn't the heart for another term as governor, she'd consider running for his job. But no; it didn't take much asking around for Hillary to see that, despite all the important work she'd done, Arkansas voters saw her only as their governor's wife.

In time, Bill regained his good spirits, and the positive energy he always got from campaigning further cheered him up. So it was that Governor Bill Clinton won his 1990 election. Then, in 1991, Bill and Hillary made the big leap, along with eleven-year-old Chelsea. On a sunny Thursday, October 3, 1991, they launched their quest for the presidency and began the biggest, most extraordinary chapter of their lives.

Hillary sparkled in a sleek cherry-red suit. Surrounded by two thousand FOBs (Friends of Bill), she looked up at the complicated fellow she'd noticed twenty-one years earlier at Yale. Now he stood, flanked by American flags, by the massive white columns of Arkansas's old statehouse. Bill Clinton thanked his "wife and friend and partner, for the love we've shared and the work she's done to make life better for the children and families of this state and this country," as he kicked off their run for the White House.

## CHAPTER 5

# RACING FOR THE PRIZE

**October 4, 1991–January 20, 1993**

Buy one, get one free.
—Bill Clinton, 1992

HILLARY AND BILL HAD ALWAYS LOVED TALKING politics. Now they positively bubbled over with ideas about improving America and, as Bill said, getting "the country ready for the future." The twenty-first century was right around the corner. But they knew that the twisting White House road was uphill all the way. For one thing, President Bush wanted to remain in office four more years. For another, many citizens liked how he had been doing his job, but they *were* worried. It was difficult for them and their government to pay the bills. The budget deficit was over $269 billion, meaning the government spent way more money than it received from people's taxes. To Bill and Hillary, that meant that the concerned and worried voters just might prefer a different president.

Maybe, with hard work and good luck, they could follow George and Barbara Bush in the long line of presidents and first ladies stretching back to George and Martha Washington. But first, Bill had to beat all the other Democratic hopefuls. In 1992 he was up against two other Democratic governors, California's Jerry Brown and Douglas Wilder of Virginia; plus two senators, Nebraska's Bob Kerrey and Tom Harkin of Iowa; Larry Agran, the ex-mayor of Irvine, California; and ex-Senator Paul Tsongas from Massachusetts. Eugene McCarthy was running again too. All but one would slip into the shadows as voters had their say in a string of events on the campaign calendar. These were the states' caucuses (local party members discussed the issues and chose their candidate) and primaries, more like regular elections.

In the early 1800s, would-be presidents met with important men and paid for nasty newspaper pieces about the other candidate. They held rallies and parades. Modern candidates need armies of helpers and millions of dollars to spread their messages across a very large country with costly TV commercials in campaigns that run at least a year and a half. Bill's 1992 campaign cost about $130 million. In 2012 Republican Mitt Romney and President Barack Obama spent more than $985 million—each.

## See How They Ran

Noble George Washington was so admired for bringing Americans through the Revolutionary War that he had little trouble becoming the first president. He was the unanimous choice. Once in office, he tried to discourage the sort of differing opinions that led to political parties. He felt they led to discord and division. But parties were forming before Washington even left office.

In the first competitive race for the presidency, in 1796, Federalist John Adams ran against Democratic-Republican Thomas Jefferson. Jefferson got fewer votes, so he became Adams's vice president. (Starting in 1804, a presidential candidate and his VP ran on the same ticket.) Campaigns became political festivals in the 1800s, complete with banners, special songs, rallies, torch-lit parades, and even free beer. Teddy Roosevelt's 1904 campaign appearances included riders on horseback and a bugler. In September and October of 1948, Harry S. Truman traveled thirty thousand miles by train, giving hundreds of "whistle-stop" speeches across America. Then, on September 28, 1960, presidential campaigns changed forever, when Americans saw John F. Kennedy and Richard Nixon debate on live television.

By February 18, 1992, the day of the first major primary, Bill and Hillary had already survived a big storm. It began January 23, with a bolt of lightning in the form of a supermarket tabloid tale in which Governor Clinton was accused of behaving inappropriately with another woman. Though Hillary hated having to talk about private business, she and Bill agreed to appear on *60 Minutes*, CBS's Sunday evening news program. If they didn't respond to the story, Bill's campaign could be sunk. The voters needed to see and hear them.

So, on January 26, right after the Super Bowl, about forty million viewers saw turquoise-clad Hillary, her blond locks secured with a black velvet headband. (To this day, style reporters make much of Hillary's hairdos.) Close beside her, Bill admitted to causing pain in his marriage. But he said to interviewer Steve Kroft, "You're looking at two people who love each other."

"You know," Hillary chimed in, "I'm not sitting here, some little woman standing by my man like Tammy Wynette. I'm sitting here because I love him and I respect him and I honor what he's been through and what we've been through together. And you know, if that's not enough for people, then heck, don't vote for him."

When she quoted Tammy Wynette's classic country song, Hillary sparked a small storm of her own by angering the singer and her fans. And she learned a strong lesson about being a national figure who had to be careful about what she said. The campaign rolled on. In that New Hampshire primary election, Bill came in second. But after his near disaster, this felt like a victory, enough to call himself "the Comeback Kid." Still, more storms lay ahead. After all, the race for the US presidency is a high-stakes game, almost like a war.

## The War Room

Up on the third floor of the old *Arkansas Gazette* newspaper building in downtown Little Rock was Clinton campaign headquarters. Hillary called it "the war room." It was a jumble of phones, fax machines, computers, TVs, piled-up desks, sleep-deprived professionals, volunteers, plus filmmakers and Hillary's friend Diane Kincaid Blair, documenting the nonstop, history-making work. Betsey Wright watched out for bad news. Bill's team had to respond quickly with its own messages, positive or negative.

Among the campaign warriors were boyish George Stephanopoulos, communications director, and James Carville, the political strategist (action planner). There was strategist Paul Begala, fund-raiser and finance manager Rahm Emanuel, and opinion-gatherer Stan Greenberg. Mandy Grunwald directed the campaign's use of TV, radio, and newspapers. They worked on Bill's ads and speeches. Then they played recordings of them for groups of voters, to get feedback and better understand their worries, such as unemployment. The campaign's message had to be that Bill Clinton could take whatever troubled Americans about their country and make it better. James Carville's famous war room sign said it this way: THE ECONOMY, STUPID.

Just after the New Hampshire primary, a new man entered the race. Plain-talking billionaire Ross Perot from Texas went on Larry King's popular CNN talk show to say that he could fix the country if only *he* was president. He had never run for political office, but voters got Perot's name on their states' ballots to make him an official independent candidate. He wanted to win votes away from Democrats and Republicans. He spent his own money to do it too—more than $63 million.

Bob Kerrey won the South Dakota primary, and then Bill won South Carolina. His Florida and Louisiana victories had him moving into the lead. To derail Clinton's momentum, at one debate Jerry Brown accused Bill of sending Arkansas's official business to the Rose Law Firm, to make Hillary rich. "I don't care what you say about me," Bill retorted, "but you ought to be ashamed of yourself for jumping on my wife. You're not worth being on the same platform as my wife."

When a reporter asked Hillary about this, she touched off another storm of protest by showing her feminist background. "You know," she responded, "I suppose I could have stayed home and baked cookies and had teas, but what I decided to do was fulfill my profession, which I entered before my husband was in public life. And I've worked very, very hard to be as careful as possible, and that's all I can tell you."

Plenty of voters zeroed in on the first part of Hillary's answer, the part that made them furious. Did Hillary disrespect women who chose to be traditional homemakers? She got so many insulting letters, editorials, and TV and radio stories that people felt sympathy for her. But Hillary had to agree with Bill's campaign advisers (and his mother) that she should appear more traditional.

Early in the campaign, Bill told voters what a great deal they'd have with him and Hillary: one vote got them two people capable of being president. They could "buy one, get one free." However, pragmatic and campaign-experienced

Hillary realized that, rather than a hardheaded copresident, the voters wanted her to be a political wife, and that was the image she'd give them. She wore softer makeup and outfits, tucked her steely mind under a new hairdo, and hid her outspoken self behind a smile.

Bill faced many questions of his own, as was proper. The people *must* know about anyone who wanted their precious vote. So they wondered if Bill had done business with Communists when he visited Russia in his student days. (No.) Did he smoke pot in the sixties? Bill said he "experimented with marijuana a time or two. . . . I didn't inhale and I didn't try it again."

Another question was more serious. Had Bill Clinton, a would-be commander in chief, dodged the draft to avoid serving his country? His 1969 letter to the commander of the University of Arkansas's ROTC program became the subject of the ABC news program *Nightline*. It showed how troubled Bill was by the Vietnam War. Many men then, such as future vice president Dick Cheney, sought deferments (rulings that let them put off or avoid service). Many others, like young Bill and President Bush's son George W., sought help from powerful friends or relatives. Bill was aided by Raymond Clinton, his politically connected step-uncle.

By June, Bill was the cool front-runner in shades, playing his saxophone on Arsenio Hall's late-night television show. On July 9, Bill announced his running mate, Tennessee senator Al Gore, another baby boomer from the South. A week later they spoke to the Democrats at the New York City convention. Next day Bill, Hillary, Al, and his wife, "Tipper" Gore set out on the first of several cross-country bus trips. More buses carried staffers, reporters, and Secret Service people. At every stop were sign-carrying voters, national and local reporters, plus lights and microphones. Cameras whirred and snapped while a security helicopter *whup-whupped* overhead.

Bill and Al signed autographs, talked, kissed babies, visited family restaurants, shook hands, struck up conversations, and chowed down on local specialties. Everywhere they went, they listened to voters' troubles with costly medical bills, insufficient insurance, or none at all. Couldn't they do *something* about America's health care system?

Bill, President Bush, and Ross Perot made many promises on their way to the live TV debates in October. Next to younger, polished Bill, with his encyclopedic brain, Perot seemed irritable and ill prepared. And in their televised Q&A with an audience of voters, President Bush was seen checking his watch. He seemed confused by a voter's poorly posed question about America's economic troubles, but Bill understood what she meant. Viewers saw him at his best, understanding, feeling, and sharing her worry.

In the last thirty hours, Hillary and Bill traveled through nine states, talking to voters from Philadelphia and Detroit to Fort Worth and Albuquerque. Bill had talked so much that, back home in Little Rock, he could barely speak. By the end of November 3, 1992, Perot had 19,741,657 votes to President Bush's 39,103,882. After nearly twelve years as Arkansas's governor, Bill Clinton received 44,909,326 votes, enough to make him the next president of the United States and Hillary the First Lady of the land.

## Earning an Electoral College Degree

Bill won 370 electoral votes to President Bush's 168. Ross Perot received none, though he won 19 percent of the popular vote (the people's votes). Confusing? Perhaps so, but this has to do with the electoral college. It's not a place, but a process: each state, plus the District of Columbia, has as many electors (selected at political parties' state conventions) as it has people in the Congress. Whoever wins a state's popular vote wins its electoral college votes. Who-ever wins the majority of *those* wins the election.

The Constitution's authors designed the electoral college for the fairest election outcome. Still, Americans have questioned the process, especially in 1824, 1876, 1888, and 2000, when four popular-vote losers won the presidency just the same: John Quincy Adams, Rutherford B. Hayes, Benjamin Harrison, and George W. Bush.

## CHAPTER 6

# HIGH HOPES AND HARD TIMES

**January 20, 1993–January 20, 1997**
There is nothing wrong with America that cannot be cured
by what is right with America.
—President Bill Clinton, January 20, 1993

Let's come together not as liberals or conservatives . . . but
as Americans who want the best for their country.
—Hillary Rodham Clinton, June 13, 1993

HILLARY CLINTON, DRESSED IN ELECTRIC BLUE, AND Tipper Gore, in vivid pink, held hands with their sober-suited husbands. A tremendous crowd of enthusiastic Democrats clapped to the campaign's song, Fleetwood Mac's "Don't Stop (Thinking About Tomorrow)." Here at last was the long-planned-for, worked-for scene in Little Rock, election night, 1992. Now the *real* work began.

Bill's presidency would start at noon on January 20, 1993. He and Hillary had seventy-eight days to pack up and prepare for the most important and meaningful jobs of their lives. Hillary and Bill had campaigned hard for more than a year and a half. Now, on the election's morning after, the dog-tired Clintons started choosing people for the Cabinet, the president's advisers.

They had help in their selections from Al Gore and Warren M. Christopher, Bill's soon-to-be secretary of state. Both men had long experience working in the nation's capital. Another team in Washington checked people's backgrounds to be sure that the Congress, special interest groups, and the public accepted their choices.

All too soon, moving vans rumbled to Washington. On January 16, 1993, Bill, Hillary, and Socks, Chelsea's black-and-white cat, left Little Rock. They, their families, and several close friends flew to meet the Gores in Char-lottesville, Virginia. After a swift, inspirational visit to Monticello, Thomas Jefferson's home, they took another bus trip together along the 121-mile route Jefferson took to Washington, DC, in 1801, but on much better roads.

They settled into Blair House, the official guesthouse across Lafayette Square from the White House. Before sunrise on the clear, cold Inauguration Day, thousands of bundled-up folks gathered along Pennsylvania Avenue to see the parade later on. More than 250,000 people packed onto the National Mall to witness the ceremony when civil power peacefully passed from one president to the next. After a prayer service at the Metropolitan African Methodist Episcopal Church, the Clintons observed one more time-honored tradition.

"Welcome to your new house," President Bush told Chelsea. He and snowy-haired Barbara and their dogs came out onto the grand North Portico of the White House to greet the new tenants of what President Gerald Ford once called "the best public housing" he'd ever seen. While the Bushes and Clintons chatted over coffee, armored limousines, Secret Service agents, and a police escort waited to take them to the Capitol.

The announcer proclaimed "Hillary Rodham Clinton" as she came to take her place. She wanted her whole name for the important work ahead. George H. W. Bush, the last presidential World War II veteran, heard "Hail to the Chief" played for him one last time. Reverend Billy Graham said a prayer. Al Gore took his oath of office. Opera star Marilyn Horne sang. The US Marine Band played. Hillary stood to witness the ceremony's key moment.

Only she knew the price she'd paid to be there. She could not know what lay ahead. For now, she held Bill's

Bible, given to him by his long-gone Arkansas grandma. Showing no sign that he'd been up nearly all night tinkering with his speech, Bill put his left hand on the Bible and raised his right, and Chief Justice William Rehnquist administered the oath of office.

Dorothy Rodham, frail, white-haired Hugh, and Bill's mom, Virginia, saw their beaming children and granddaughter Chelsea exchange quick kisses. They and millions of others heard poet and civil rights activist Maya Angelou read her special inauguration poem. After the national anthem, after a helicopter whisked the Bushes up and away, came the traditional Capitol luncheon and inaugural parade. President Clinton, his Secret Service detail, and the new First Lady walked part of it.

Chelsea, her friends, her mom, and her grandmothers took advantage of the salon on the White House's second floor. It was there thanks to President Nixon's wife, Pat. They were "transformed," Hillary remembered, "like Cinderellas, for the balls." Eleven inaugural balls. She glittered in a blue-violet gown of beaded lace and silk velvet. Bill turned from their dance to ask the cheering crowd, "Is Hillary beautiful tonight, or what?" Indeed she was.

Just as Hillary had tried to redefine the role of First

Lady of Arkansas, so too did she attempt to remake the position of First Lady of the United States.

## First Ladies

Not until the 1800s did the term "First Lady" come into general use, but there has always been one. Proper etiquette dictated that George's wife, Martha Washington, be there to help greet his official guests. Claudia "Lady Bird" Johnson, wife of the thirty-sixth president, said that the First Lady is "an unpaid public servant elected by one person, her husband." Still, Lady Bird and many presidential wives have stood out in history. Abigail Adams was the first to occupy the White House. Frances Cleveland was the only First Lady to be married there, to the twenty-second president. The twenty-eighth president's wife, Edith Wilson, took on many of her husband's official tasks after his debilitating stroke.

If the president had no wife, others stepped into the role. Dolley Madison, wife of the fourth president, served as official hostess for their widowed friend, third president Thomas Jefferson. As did Harriet Lane, for her bachelor uncle, fifteenth president James Buchanan. And some presidents outlived their first wives, so they married a second First Lady. Hillary was First Lady number fifty-three.

For advice on being a White House mom, Hillary visited the thirty-fifth president's widow, Jacqueline Kennedy Onassis. The two became good friends, but of all the first ladies, Hillary most admired

Eleanor Roosevelt, wife of thirty-second president Franklin D. Roosevelt. Because FDR was wheelchair-bound, Eleanor traveled the world for him. She visited American troops stationed overseas in World War II, wrote a popular daily newspaper column, and invited female reporters to the White House to conduct her own press conferences—a First Lady first. All this, plus her work for the young United Nations, earned Mrs. Roosevelt her own often controversial identity as First Lady of the World.

The White House has about a hundred people on permanent staff, including cooks, gardeners, and such. Each administration has its own staff. Here, the Clintons definitely wanted people they knew and trusted, so they picked George Stephanopoulos for communications director. For his chief of staff, Bill chose business executive Thomas "Mack" McLarty, whom he'd known since kindergarten. Hillary wanted Vince Foster and Webb Hubbell for deputy White House counsel (legal adviser) and associate attorney general, respectively.

For her own staff chief, Hillary picked her Children's Defense Fund colleague, Maggie Williams. Her tiny office and Hillary's would be upstairs from the Oval Office. No First Lady had *ever* had her office in the White House's West Wing. She and Bill intended to work closely together, as always. The rest of her staff (twenty in all) would work in the East Wing and in the grand Old Executive Office Building. Together, the staff would be known as Hillary-land. They'd help her oversee domestic programs plus the correspondence and scheduling that went with being First Lady.

Traditionally, a new administration gets a honeymoon period, time to settle in before the harsh criticism begins. But the Clinton team seemed to hit the ground staggering, attacked from all sides.

"A lot of the mistakes we made in the first weeks were because we were so tired," George Stephanopoulos remembered. Other missteps had to do with how little Bill, Hillary, and their friends were prepared for life in the White House and for Washington's hardball, pressure-cooker politics. As for reporters, they were long accustomed to going directly from the oft-televised Briefing Room over to the West Wing to pick up information. Hillary didn't trust the press corps to be fair so she ordered their hallway blocked (a decision she later reversed). And reporters were warned not to bother Chelsea over at Sidwell Friends, her new private school.

The angry journalists unleashed loads of questions

about the new president's troubles. For one thing, there were problems with the women he and Hillary initially chose to serve as attorney general. Not until March 12 did Janet Reno become the AG. For another, President Clinton faced a protest buzz saw when he tried to allow gay people to serve openly in the military.

Only slightly less controversial was the announcement he made just five days into his presidency. Hillary, a serious, longtime public servant, was eager to remedy the people's need for proper medical care. On January 25, 1993, the president said that he was appointing his wife to head his Task Force on National Health Care Reform.

It wasn't as if America's medical system didn't need fixing. Some 37 million citizens were uninsured, and ever-rising medical costs dragged down the economy. But Hillary's project was troubled from the very beginning.

By law, the president's family cannot be government employees, so the idea of the First Lady overseeing such a gigantic, complex, official legislation project upset some voters and lawmakers. Hillary admitted that she wasn't a health care expert, but she was confident in her intellect and experience. With her business consultant friend Ira Maga-ziner and five hundred experts, she could surely hammer out a way for the government and private insurance companies to provide people with basic, affordable medical benefits.

To limit confusion from too many outside arguments, Hillary closed her meetings to the public and inquisitive reporters. Many hated such secrecy. The powerful insurance industry objected to reforms that might hurt their profits. Other voters and lawmakers balked at the possibility of "socialized medicine." Congressional Democrats, whose support Hillary would need, feared political damage if she presented her program before 1994's midterm election. They asked her to delay, but she refused. In the midst of this stressful situation, Hillary got a phone call.

Another stroke had put Hugh Rodham into a coma. Hillary, her brothers, and Chelsea rushed to Little Rock to sit with Dorothy at Hugh's bedside. His respirator clicked and whirred. "I smoothed his hair and spoke to him," Hillary wrote later on. Her eighty-two-year-old dad died on April 7, 1993. On top of this sorrow, Bill found out that his mother was sick with the cancer that would take her life nine months later, in January 1994.

Back in Washington, Hillary found comfort by joining other women in their prayer group. Besides her personal grief, she was managing the gigantic task of reforming the country's health care delivery system while having her words and work constantly questioned by the press and politicians. Plus, there was the loss of privacy that came with life in the White House. Her family's home was a workplace as well, watched over by ever-present Secret Service agents.

In one of the White House's busy offices, workers arranged trips for President Clinton, other officials, and reporters. Concerned that these staffers might be mismanaging the money they handled, Hillary asked her trusted counsel, Vince Foster, to look into it. Unwittingly, this launched a series of events that led to investigations, staffers being fired, and a media firestorm that erupted around the scandal known as "Travelgate." Dignified Vince, who'd silently suffered the relentless pressure of his work, now had his character and ability questioned in the press. On July 20, 1993, he took his own life, which resulted in suggestions that Foster knew too much about the Clintons' Arkansas past. But Hillary boxed away her hurt and steeled herself to work. She and Bill had to sell their health care plan to the nation.

President Clinton presented it in a stirring speech to the Congress. Six days later, September 28, 1993, Hillary too went to Capitol Hill. Worn thin by sorrow, the polished

First Lady went before dozens of photographers, representatives, and senators to testify at five congressional committees, "as an American citizen concerned about the health of her family and the health of her nation."

It quickly became clear that studious, passionate Hillary knew every detail of the Health Security Act bill, the complex set of laws her task force proposed. Afterward, she traveled throughout America speaking for her plan, but it was very difficult for ordinary citizens to grasp a complicated bill 1,342 pages long. Hillary's audiences were full of citizens who'd heard and seen all the anti-reform ads and speeches in the media.

Crowds booed her and shouted insults. Hillary herself hurt her cause with her unwillingness to compromise. In the end, her and Bill's high hopes for reforming health care failed in September 1994 because of lack of support—just when another political storm swirled around their heads: Whitewater.

## Whitewater

In 1978 Hillary and Bill, along with Jim and Susan McDougal, had hoped that buying that northern Arkansas land would be a smart investment, but instead they lost money. Later the McDougals bought a savings and loan company. Later still, they were suspected of illegally using the depositors' money to settle their own Whitewater losses.

McDougal took his legal troubles to the Rose Law Firm, in which Hillary and Vince Foster were partners. After Vince died, more questions arose. As the First Lady's lawyer, he'd had her old Rose Law Firm files, but now they were missing. Investigators and reporters wanted to check them to see how Hillary had handled McDougal's dealings and if she and Bill had profited from them. When Hillary couldn't find her records and wouldn't release the files she had, Republicans and even some Democrats demanded that an independent counsel investigate.

Hillary begged Bill to stand firm, but the political pressure got to him. In January 1994, two weeks after his mom died, exactly one year after becoming president, Bill asked AG Janet Reno to appoint a special prosecutor. She chose Robert Fiske. The Whitewater investigation revealed that Hillary's friend Webb Hubbell had stolen money from the Rose Law Firm. (He resigned from the Clinton administration and spent eighteen months in prison.) When Fiske found no specific White House wrongdoings, the Republicans found a lawyer they liked better, in August 1994. Conservative Ken Starr's investigation would go far beyond Arkansas real estate.

Regardless of his and Hillary's Washington troubles, President Clinton had to deal with the world. His predecessor,

President Bush, had sent American troops to help famine victims in Somalia. In a battle there in late 1993, Somalis shot down two Black Hawk helicopters and killed eighteen US soldiers. President Clinton pulled the troops out. All too aware of how angry Americans were after that African disaster, he didn't send help when Rwanda's Hutu people killed some eight hundred thousand of their Tutsi countrymen. He was also resisting Europeans demands for American help to stop a horrific civil war in Bosnia, in southern Europe. But he did travel with Hillary to the Middle East to oversee an Israel-Jordan peace agreement.

When her forty-seventh birthday dawned on October 26, 1994, Hillary was in Egypt. One can only imagine her thoughts as she watched the morning light on the ancient pyramids of Giza. She'd suffered so many losses. Another big one came in the '94 midterm elections, when Americans voted so many Democrats out of office that the Republicans won control of the House *and* the Senate for the first time in forty years. It was a tremendous political defeat for the Clintons, and Hillary took it hard. She wondered what her hero, Eleanor Roosevelt, would do.

Hillary decided to follow Eleanor's example. Like ER, she traveled. As First Lady, Hillary visited eighty-two countries. Chelsea came along on one of her mother's journeys, to South Asia, during which Hillary experienced a turning point in her troubled life.

Hillary and fifteen-year-old Chelsea visited women's health clinics. They enjoyed a mother-daughter elephant ride in Nepal. Hillary met with Pakistan's female prime minister, Benazir Bhutto. In India, Hillary and Chelsea attended a meeting of the Self-Employed Women's Association. With small loans, training, and encouragement, SEWA helped vendors and craftswomen struggle up from wretched poverty. Hillary and her daughter listened as hundreds of them sang "We Shall Overcome" in their native language. Their courage and optimism opened Hillary's tear-filled eyes to a wider world full of problems larger than her own.

In April 1995, not long after Hillary's Asian journey, US terrorists bombed Oklahoma City's federal building, killing 168 people. Americans were warmed by President Clinton's strong compassion for the victims' families. In the months thereafter, Hillary reached out to Americans in a weekly syndicated newspaper column, *Talking It Over*. She began writing a book too, about the social support systems children need besides their parents, teachers, grandparents, and good schools. Hillary took her title, *It Takes a Village*, from an African proverb: "It takes a village to raise a child." Then, in September, she brought a powerful message to the world.

Specifically, in China, at the United Nations Fourth World Conference on Women, Hillary spoke about the deadly cruelties and sexual violence experienced by so many of the world's women and girls. "It is time for us to say here in Beijing, and the world to hear, that it is no longer acceptable to discuss women's rights as separate from human rights," she proclaimed. "For too long, the history of women has been a history of silence. Even today, there are those who are trying to silence our words."

Truly, Chinese officials blocked her speech from official TV and radio stations, and after Hillary spoke, her listeners from 189 nations sat silent. But the instant her translated words streamed through their headphones, they leaped to their feet to applaud and cheer America's First Lady. She was cheered, too, on the *New York Times* editorial page: her speech "may have been her finest moment in public life."

As First Lady, Hillary failed to change the American way of health care. She couldn't stop the Senate Republicans'

Whitewater investigations or their endless demands for documents (particularly her misplaced Rose Law Firm files), but there were things that she could do, such as working with AG Janet Reno to form the Justice Department's Office on Violence Against Women. And in distant China, she had found her voice as a champion for the world's women and girls. "We share a common future," said Hillary at Beijing. "And we are here to find common ground so that we may help bring new dignity and respect to women and girls all over the world—and in so doing, bring new strength and stability to families as well."

All the while, President Clinton was struggling to find a way to end that thorny war in Bosnia. In Washington, he dealt with the strong ideological differences between his administration and the conservative congressional Republicans. They so objected to big, costly government solutions to Americans' problems that, for a while in 1995, they basically shut down the government by denying funding to federal facilities, such as national parks and museums. Thousands of angry government employees were locked out of their jobs, unpaid. When Bill Clinton refused to compromise, the Republicans (minus much of their popularity) were forced to reopen the government.

By January 1996, the economy was growing and generating more jobs. Hillary, whose book was about to be published, had earned back much of the public approval she'd lost in the health care battles. But then, one of her aides found those Rose Law Firm files, misplaced in a White House closet.

Hands shaking, Hillary gave them to her lawyers, who turned them over to the investigators. She knew that on the other side of America's liberal/conservative divide, there would be citizens who'd believe that she'd had them all along, that she hadn't been truthful.

Now the special prosecutor, Ken Starr, sent a message to Hillary. He was ordering the First Lady to come to court and testify about the records and anything else he needed to know. If she didn't, he would charge her with criminal perjury (lying) and standing in the way of justice.

It was an angry, anxious time for Hillary and her husband. Nevertheless, it wasn't long before Hillary was championing an official effort to discover why so many Gulf War veterans returned from their service in Iraq with digestive and breathing problems as well as other ailments. And, despite all the troubles swirling around the Clinton White House, millions more Americans had jobs; and the huge budget deficit was cut in half. President Clinton signed a law to raise the minimum wage from $4.25 per hour to $5.15. And he pleased conservative voters by signing the 1996 Welfare Reform Act. But liberal Democrats, such as Hillary's old friend Ms. Edelman, were deeply upset by the law's requirement that underprivileged people receiving benefits work at least twenty hours weekly. Nevertheless, Bill Clinton defeated Republican senator Bob Dole on November 5, 1996. Not since Franklin D. Roosevelt, in 1936, had a Democrat won a second term. Despite everything, Hillary and Bill had four more years in the White House.

## CHAPTER 7

# FOUR MORE YEARS

**January 20, 1997–January 20, 2001**

Progress depends on the choices we make today for tomorrow and on whether we meet our challenges and protect our values.
—Hillary Rodham Clinton, August 27, 1996

HILLARY WAS DETERMINED TO KEEP DOING WHAT she could to improve families' lives. Early in her second term as First Lady, she hosted a White House conference concerning the ways very young children develop and learn. She followed this with another devoted to the particular needs of young Latinas and Latinos. Besides helping Bill to entertain visiting dignitaries at glittering state dinners, Hillary launched a childhood reading campaign and pushed to save the National Endowment for the Humanities from being defunded by congressional Republicans. In addition to her work for a law that would help federal and state governments provide poor children with medical insurance, she championed 1997's Adoption and Safe Families Act, which helped foster families adopt children with special needs.

Meanwhile, President Clinton and Congress agreed on a budget. With this plan and the era's strong economy, the government soon had a surplus, more money than it needed. Bill also helped Ireland's warring Protestants and Catholics make peace.

In President Clinton's free time at rustic Camp David, the presidential getaway in Maryland, Secret Service agents let him use one of their official cars to teach teenage Chelsea how to drive. There and at the White House, the Clintons played with Buddy, their new chocolate Labrador retriever puppy. He'd be company for Chelsea's parents and take some of the sting out of their only child leaving for college. Starting in fall 1997, Chelsea Clinton would be a freshman at Stanford University in Palo Alto, California. Perhaps it was fortunate that Hillary and Bill's treasured daughter was moving three time zones away, considering the political troubles that lay ahead for her parents.

Since 1994, independent counsel Ken Starr and his investigators had been looking into the Clintons' dealings with their Arkansas friends, before and during Bill's presidency. The investigation of Jim and Susan McDougal, Hillary and Bill's partners in the Whitewater real estate deal, led to the McDougals' imprisonment for banking illegalities. (Jim died in prison in 1998.) Susan was also jailed for refusing to talk to a federal grand jury. Mr. Starr's team did not find enough evidence to try the Clintons for Whitewater wrongdoings, but in early 1998, Starr got word of improper activities in the White House involving a female government employee. He began investigating President Clinton's personal conduct.

When news of this reached the public, a scandal erupted, and on January 27, 1998, Hillary appeared on NBC's *Today* show. She told television host Matt Lauer that the "great story here, for anybody willing to find it and write about it and explain it, is this vast right-wing conspiracy that has been conspiring against my husband since the day he announced for president."

Certainly there were citizens and pundits who disagreed with her, but to Hillary, it was clear that she and Bill were at the center of a political war of words. It was particularly heated in the nation's capital, but it extended to many an American dinner table. Over the decades since the Vietnam War, she'd seen how voters on the conserva-

Belva Ann Lockwood was a women's rights activist, a lawyer, and the first woman to argue a case in front of the Supreme Court.

First Lady Eleanor Roosevelt delivers a radio message to the American people during World War II.

Republican presidential candidate Senator Barry Goldwater arrives in Chicago for a campaign event in February 1964.

Hillary Rodham at Wellesley College in the late 1960s.

Demonstrators at the Federal Building in Chicago in support of the Chicago 8, who were on trial for conspiring to promote riots at the 1968 Democratic National Convention.

Marchers in support of the Panther 21, members of the Black Panthers arrested by New York police under suspicion of planning a series of bombings. The charges against all the defendants were eventually dropped.

Betty Friedan (standing in center of photo) was a leading figure in the women's liberation movement, a bestselling author, and a cofounder of the National Organization for Women (NOW).

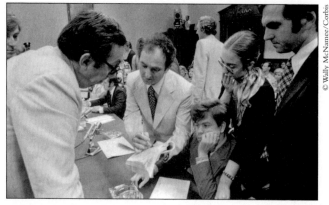

Hillary Rodham was a member of the presidential impeachment inquiry staff during the Watergate scandal.

Bill and Hillary Clinton after casting their votes in the 1982 Arkansas gubernatorial election.

Hillary, Bill, and Chelsea Clinton after Bill wins the Democratic nomination for president in 1992.

Hillary Clinton with her mother, Dorothy Rodham, in 1992.

First Lady Hillary Clinton holds a press conference about the Whitewater controversy.

In Seattle, Washington, First Lady Hillary Clinton presents her health care plan.

Hillary and Chelsea Clinton visit an orphanage in India run by Mother Teresa, on a three-day visit to India as part of a South Asia tour.

Senator Hillary Clinton at a press conference at Ground Zero, speaking about increasing funding for those with health problems related to the 9/11 terrorist attacks.

President Obama, Vice President Biden, Secretary of State Clinton, and members of the national security team receive an update on the mission against Osama bin Laden in the Situation Room of the White House in 2011.

Hillary, Chelsea, and Bill Clinton with Graça Machel, widow of Nelson Mandela, at the 2014 Clinton Global Initiative meeting.

Tunisians demonstrating in Tunis against terrorism, following an attack on the Bardo museum.

Democratic presidential candidates Bernie Sanders and Hillary Clinton debate at Saint Anselm College in Manchester, New Hampshire, in December 2015.

tive right and those on the liberal left had become more divided—and all the more so as they turned to online and cable news sources that reflected their points of view. It seemed to her that powerful conservatives were determined to sink the Clinton administration any way they could.

Americans generally approved of how their nation was progressing during Bill Clinton's presidency. But they did become upset with him as Mr. Starr's investigation proceeded and their president was forced to answer personal questions about his private life. As for Hillary, whatever failings her husband possessed, she decided to let them live alongside her love for him and all that was good and great about Bill Clinton. After all, as she would write later, "no one understands me better."

A curious side effect of the Clintons' well-publicized troubles was Hillary's increased popularity. The general public who didn't like her as a political warrior for health care reform loved her as a First Lady who maintained her dignity even as she weathered a personal and political crisis.

On September 9, 1998, after almost five years and more than 50 million dollars' worth of investigation, the Office of the Independent Counsel sent thirty-six boxes of evidence to the House of Representatives. The 445-page Starr Report was released two days later. In it, Mr. Starr laid out his case against President Clinton, saying, among other things, that he'd interfered with witnesses and abused his power. On October 8, after the House Judiciary Committee, then the entire House, went over the evidence, they voted to debate the president's case. On December 19, 1998, the House voted along party lines to impeach President Clinton. The Republicans, mostly, charged him with obstructing justice and lying under oath to a grand jury.

As a young lawyer, Hillary had worked on President Nixon's impeachment proceedings. She knew that Bill's wrongdoings certainly didn't stand up to "treason, bribery, or other high crimes and misdemeanors," the Constitution's reasons for impeachment. But Bill's fate was sealed. He had to face a trial before the US Senate. In 1974, President Nixon had resigned rather than face impeachment and a Senate trial. Not so for President Clinton. As much as he regretted his mistakes, he was not going to quit and be done in by "the politics of personal destruction."

So, on January 7, 1999, 111 years after the nation's only other such trial (for President Andrew Johnson), the trial of President William Jefferson Clinton was under way. His judge was the man who'd sworn him into office, Chief Justice William Rehnquist. Mindful of the high occasion, he had golden stripes sewn onto the sleeves of his black judicial robe. He'd hear the evidence along with the senators.

As the senators up on Capitol Hill decided on her husband's guilt or innocence. Hillary was in the White House, planning a future of her own.

# CHAPTER 8

# THE SENATOR FROM NEW YORK

**January 3, 2001–January 21, 2009**
I suppose the questions on everyone's mind are:
Why the Senate? Why New York? And why me?
—Hillary Rodham Clinton, July 7, 1999

TO CONVICT PRESIDENT CLINTON, TWO-THIRDS OF the senators had to vote him guilty. As it happened, they didn't. When the trial ended February 12, 1999, Bill Clinton had survived.

Hillary still had nearly two years left before she and Bill left the White House, but what then? Her admirers thought she might take charge of a foundation, a corporation, or a college or even host a TV talk show—an idea that Hillary quickly rejected. Then there was news: the distinguished Democratic New York senator Daniel Patrick Moynihan said he was not running for reelection in 2000. What if Hillary ran for his job? her friends wondered.

**90**

In February 1999, Hillary and Harold Ickes, the president's deputy chief of staff, were poring over a large map of the state of New York. Ickes was an expert on tough New York politics. He had lots of good reasons why the First Lady's run for the Senate was not a good idea.

Hillary Clinton, who'd never run for political office, would have to drum up at least $25 million for a campaign in New York, where no woman had ever won a statewide election. She would have to cover the Empire State's more than 54,000 square miles (140,000 square kilometers), convincing nearly twenty million citizens (including a *very* tough press corps) that she could represent them in the US Senate even though she had never lived in New York. She'd need to know the state's history, industries, ethnic groups, unions, and towns full of people hurting from all the lost manufacturing jobs. That wasn't even counting New York City's boroughs: Brooklyn, Queens, Staten Island, the Bronx, and Manhattan. More than likely, she'd be running against New York City mayor Rudolph Giuliani, a fierce anti-Clinton Republican. And while she campaigned, she'd still be First Lady. The job had its own set of demanding duties besides those that Hillary took on, like persuading Congress to pass the Foster Care

Independence Act in 1999. It allowed young people to get the help they needed as they turned eighteen, too old for foster care.

Hillary considered all of Ickes's objections, but what were her strengths? For one, she knew herself to be an excellent, industrious student. For another, she had high approval ratings; plus, she was pretty fierce herself. Hillary was a strong, smart woman who wanted to serve the public independently, in her own right. Besides, like everyone in her generation, Hillary well remembered when non–New Yorker Bobby Kennedy became a New York senator in 1964, then ran for president four years later.

As for Bill Clinton, he knew that a third term as president was against US law. He could follow the example of the sixth president, John Quincy Adams, who served in the House of Representatives after he left the White House in 1829. But after President Clinton left office on January 20, 2001, he likely would not run for public office again. For him and Hillary, just talking together about a possible political campaign lit up the lights that had first attracted them to each other. Ever the savvy politician, Bill encouraged Hillary. Hadn't she given up a promising career to support his ambitions? Bill promised to coach and support Hillary in her campaign. Four days after her meeting with Harold Ickes, the First Lady's office issued a statement: she was considering a run for the US Senate.

On July 7, 1999, some two hundred reporters came to Senator Moynihan's farm in upstate New York to cover her official announcement.

"I intend to be spending my time in the next days and weeks and months listening to New Yorkers," she said. "I care deeply about the issues that are important in this state, that I've already been learning about and hearing about."

Just as she'd done to become student president at Wellesley and when she pushed for Arkansas's education reform, Hillary now set out to discover what New Yorkers wanted. She climbed into her Ford van, known as the "HRC Speedwagon," and set off on a "listening tour" to interview voters. In her spare time, she and Bill went house hunting. The Clintons owed their lawyers as much as $4 million, but they managed to borrow money for an eleven-room, $1.7 million house in Chappaqua, New York.

In the next hectic months, between listening and

learning all she could about her new home state, Hillary went with Bill more than once back to their old one. In Fayetteville, Arkansas, they spent time with Hillary's dear friend, Diane Kincaid Blair. When she had married lawyer and futures trader Jim Blair, Governor Clinton had performed the ceremony and Hillary had been their "best person." Later Diane had made many notes and conducted interviews for the book she meant to write about the '92 campaign and the Clintons' difficult White House years. For example, she recorded her friend Hillary's impatience, in July 1993, with trying to make Washington's "insane process" work. Now Hillary was campaigning hard to make an important place for herself in it.

She didn't have Bill's golden gift of easygoing gab, but she had confidence in her knowledge and ideas. Unlike her husband, Hillary wasn't a natural at connecting with people, but she was tough enough to go out every day, smile, shake hands, and speak her piece. "My God," she'd exclaim, "Bill made it look so easy!"

She tried not to offend any New Yorkers, but they doubted Hillary's authenticity when the Chicago-born candidate donned a Yankees ball cap, claiming to be a fan. (Young Hillary had rooted for the Cubs, but she really did admire handsome Yankee Mickey Mantle.) And when she went to Israel as First Lady and exchanged a polite air-kiss with the wife of Palestinian leader Yasir Arafat, Jewish New Yorkers were not pleased.

Still, Hillary kept smiling, soldiered on, and won the nomination. As for her opponent, ill health and other personal issues forced Mayor Giuliani to drop out of the race. Now the Republicans picked young New York congressman Rick Lazio to oppose Mrs. Clinton. This he did, enthusiastically.

Lazio had made an issue of all the soft money (anonymous contributions) pouring into the nation's political campaigns. At a televised debate, Lazio challenged Hillary to sign his "New York Freedom from Soft Money Pact." He left his podium and waved the document in her face, but his tough act backfired. To many female viewers, Lazio looked like a bully. And on November 7, 2000, Hillary became the only First Lady ever to be elected to the US Senate. President Clinton stood in the background at his wife's New York City celebration. Bill's eyes glistened as he and Chelsea beamed proud smiles at Hillary, in a turquoise pantsuit. Before a cheering crowd, she gloried in her victory.

"Sixty-two counties, sixteen months, three debates, two opponents, and six black pantsuits later, because of you, here we are!"

## A Woman's Place in US Politics

In the long, curious, often painful history of the relationship between American women and their government, there are many key moments. Elizabeth Cady Stanton didn't have the right to vote, but in 1866, she was the first woman to run for a seat in the US House of Representatives. She got only twelve votes, but hers was a brave effort. Women who have run for public office have had to get past people who simply weren't used to seeing women in high positions of authority. Merely *voting* was enough to get Mrs. Stanton's friend Susan B. Anthony arrested. That was in 1872, the year Victoria Woodhull ran for president, a female first.

America's first woman mayor was Susanna Salter of Argonia, Kansas, in 1887. Then, in 1916, when Montanans elected Jeannette Rankin, she became the first US congresswoman. No Latina had ever won a statewide election—until Soledad Chacón became New Mexico's secretary of state in 1923. Wyoming's Nellie Tayloe Ross became the first female governor in 1925. Hattie Wyatt Caraway of Arkansas took over her husband's Senate seat when he died in 1931, but in 1932, she was elected in her own right—another in the long list of many firsts for women.

The results of the 2000 presidential election were not so definite. Al Gore won the popular vote, but there was a long, angry argument over the electoral votes. On December 12, the US Supreme Court settled it. Five conservative justices stopped a questionable vote recount in the key state of Florida, making Texas governor George W. Bush the new president-elect.

Four days later, Senator-Elect Clinton was offered $8 million to write *Living History*, a book about her life, including her stormy years in the White House. Only Pope John Paul II had ever received more, in 1994, for his nonfiction book. Hillary used part of her money ($2,850,000) to buy a house in Washington, DC. "Whitehaven" would be her fund-raising and political headquarters, as well as a home for her, Bill (when he was in town), and eighty-one-year-old Dorothy Rodham.

On January 3, 2001, First Lady Hillary Rodham Clinton and her Secret Service detail traveled the sixteen blocks from the White House to the Capitol. President Clinton, Chelsea, and Hillary's mom watched from the visitors' gallery as Vice President Al Gore administered the oath of office for the new freshman senator from New York. Tourists asked for her autograph. They and reporters snapped pictures of Senator Hillary Clinton (D–NY), meaning now she was an official Democrat from New York.

Hillary *was* a celebrity, but she knew better than to act like one. Around the ninety-nine other senators, Hillary conducted herself as a friendly professional, one willing to fetch coffee for her colleagues. She showed up, well prepared, for votes and hearings. She worked on legislation with other Democrats and with Republicans, including those who'd worked against the Clinton presidency. Eager to learn, Hillary called on the man most knowledgeable of the Senate's ways and customs: the dapper West Virginia Democrat, Senator Robert Byrd. Hillary was determined to win respect and do a good job for New Yorkers. "A workhorse," a colleague soon described her, "not a show horse."

On his last day as president, Bill Clinton officially pardoned his half brother, Roger Clinton, who'd been imprisoned for dealing drugs, and Susan McDougal, who'd gone to jail rather than speak against him; but not Webb Hubbell, jailed for tax problems and overbilling the Rose Law Firm back in Little Rock. Then, at the end, before they welcomed George and Laura Bush to their new home, Bill took Hillary in his arms for a waltz around the old mansion's polished marble hallway.

On the bright blue morning of September 11, 2001, nine months into her term of office, Senator Clinton was in DC on her way to the Capitol when she heard awful news from New York City. Like nearly everyone, she figured that a plane had accidentally flown into one of the World Trade Center towers—until a second passenger airliner struck seventeen minutes later. And, like everyone else who happened to have a dear one in Manhattan, both of Chelsea Clinton's parents were frantic until they heard she was safe.

Even as Hillary and others in the Capitol watched the frightful TV pictures, they were rushed to safer locations. Another plane had flown into the Defense Department's headquarters, the Pentagon. A fourth aircraft had been aiming for yet another target (the White House? the Capitol?) when it crashed on its way to Washington. Before the dreadful day ended, Hillary stood with about 150 other members of Congress on the East Front steps of the Capitol, singing, "God bless America, land that I love . . ."

In the next days, Hillary talked long on the phone with

ex-President Clinton, her chief adviser. Any country that chose to harbor terrorists, she declared in the Senate, "will now face the wrath of our country." She and fellow New York senator Charles Schumer went to meet with Mayor Giuliani and other officials at the still-smoking scene of the crime in New York City's downtown financial district. They paid their respects to the more than 2,700 innocents who had died there.

Back in DC, Senator Clinton met with President Bush to help obtain $21 billion in federal aid for New York City's recovery and rebuilding. She worked to see that there was medical treatment for the firefighters, police, and other first responders to the dusty, dangerous 9/11 disaster. But how should the United States respond to the attacks? That was the question.

The terrorists who had carried out the deadly attacks were followers of Osama bin Laden, a Saudi Arabian leader of an extreme form of Islam. Soon President Bush ordered US forces into Afghanistan, where bin Laden was based. Additionally, the president and his team were determined to topple the vile dictator of Iraq, Saddam Hussein.

Some of Hillary's Congressional colleagues, such as

Senator Robert Byrd and Vermont Representative Bernie Sanders, objected to the Iraq War Resolution. But Senator Clinton joined the majority that voted October 10, 2002, to give President Bush the authority to do what he thought necessary to wage war on terrorism, even using military force in Iraq. It was a vote she would later regret, but at the time, she was rewarded with a rare prize for a first-term senator: the chance to serve on the powerful Armed Services Committee. Hillary already served on the Health and Budget committees, as well as those for Education, Labor, and Pensions; Environment and Public Works; and the Special Committee on Aging. With her new assignment, Hillary learned more about the military. Generals came to respect her as a knowledgeable lawmaker, who'd work and speak up for such things as better armor for American troops.

Four hellish years or so and thousands of US and Iraqi deaths later, Hillary was running for a second Senate term in 2006. By then, the poorly planned Iraq War had become very unpopular. Senator Clinton and others spoke of letting US forces leave Iraq, little by little, but many a voter looked down on those, such as Hillary, who'd voted in 2002 to authorize the war. "Obviously," she said later on

the *Today* show, "if we knew then what we know now ...
I certainly wouldn't have voted that way."

Nevertheless, New Yorkers could see what an effective,
important, and admirable senator they had in Hillary. She'd
worked hard to protect their jobs and create more of them.
Besides visiting US troops in Afghanistan and in Iraq, she
worked to improve veterans' health benefits. Throughout
Senator Clinton's successful reelection campaign, she and
her staff, her Hillaryland-on-Capitol-Hill, attended to
lawmaking. From extending unemployment insurance to
the jobless to seeing that women were paid as well as their
male coworkers to helping rural New Yorkers get broad-
band access, they were busy—but not so busy that they
weren't mindful of the future. Just beyond the horizon lay
the 2008 presidential election, coming Hillary's way.

CHAPTER 9

# CRACKS IN THE CEILING

**2007–2008**
I'm in. And I'm in to win.
—Hillary Rodham Clinton, January 20, 2007

TO HER CLASSMATES AT WELLESLEY COLLEGE, smart, hardworking Hillary seemed the one most likely to break through America's ultimate "glass ceiling," the invisible barrier between women and their nation's highest office. Now world-famous, powerful Senator Clinton was the most likely politician to win the Democratic presidential nomination. On January 20, 2007, exactly two years before her Inauguration Day (she hoped), Hillary appeared in a video on her website, announcing her intention to do just that. "I'm not just starting a campaign, though. I'm beginning a conversation, with you, with America."

## Women Who Sought the Top Job

At thirty-one, journalist/stockbroker Victoria Woodhull was four years shy of the age set forth in the Constitution for a US president. It would be almost fifty years before American women could even vote for one, but she declared her official candidacy on April 2, 1870. In 1884 lawyer/suffragist Belva Lockwood of the National Equal Rights Party ran too. The Republicans were the first major party to place a woman in nomination for the presidency in 1964, but Senator Margaret Chase Smith lost to young Hillary's favorite, Senator Goldwater. Democratic Congresswomen Patsy Takemoto Mink and Shirley Chisholm were presidential candidates in 1972, as was Ellen McCormack in 1976. Sonia Johnson ran as a third-party candidate in 1984, the year Geraldine Ferraro ran as the Dems' vice-presidential candidate. Socialist Lenora Fulani and Democratic congresswoman Patricia Schroeder both ran in 1988. Elizabeth Dole, in 1999, then Carol Moseley Braun, in 2004, had presidential campaigns—very brief ones compared to the marathon Hillary Rodham Clinton conducted in 2008. She brings many lessons learned to her 2016 campaign.

Unfortunately for Hillary, in 2008 America seemed to be listening to someone else. In early 2004, few knew about Barack Obama of Chicago, biracial son of an adventurous Kansas anthropologist and an economist from Kenya.

Then, on July 27, 2004, this forty-two-year-old US Senate candidate captured worldwide attention with an electrifying speech at the Democrats' National Convention. Americans, fed up and frustrated with their static, party-divided government, loved Obama speaking of the "politics of hope." Hating all the arguing between "blue" Democrats and "red" Republicans, they loved his idealistic talk of a unified America.

In 2005 Mr. Obama, the newly elected senator from Illinois, sought out Senator Clinton. He admired Hillary's strength and know-how. When asked, she was happy to advise him. He should do as she'd done: Don't be distracted by the fame game. (She was an expert on that.) Study to be well prepared in committees, where he could do important work for the voters who'd sent him to Washington.

Throughout 2006, while Hillary worked on legislation, encouraged New Yorkers to reelect her, and considered a possible presidential run, Obama's popularity soared. Besides his own work in the Senate, Barack Obama was touring to promote his 2006 bestseller, *The Audacity of Hope*. In the crowds that turned out to see and hear him, citizens called for him to run for president.

President Bush's approval ratings had dropped since the 9/11 attacks of 2001. The costly Afghanistan and Iraq wars were wearing down Americans' spirits. They were not happy with the government's less-than-effective response when Hurricane Katrina struck New Orleans in 2005. The US economy seemed to be losing strength in 2007. The banks were foreclosing on more and more homes. No wonder wary Americans were looking for change. Even Obama's fellow senators told him (behind Hillary's back, fearing her anger and disappointment) that he should run, now, before he built up a troublesome voting record like Hillary's (her 2002 vote for President Bush's Iraq policy, for example).

Hillary had earned respect in the Senate, even from her former enemies, but conservative voters were still against her and her politics. Democrats were wary of her "baggage," the dramas that swirled around her and her husband. Bill Clinton had made a good recovery after doctors opened his chest in 2004, to fix blocked veins in his heart. But how would former President Clinton handle being back in the White House as his wife's First Gentleman?

Hillary was impressed with Senator Obama, but did she see him as a threat to her presidential ambitions? Certainly not—this was her time. With all the work she'd done and money she'd raised for the Democrats, she'd *earned* it! To Hillary, her friend Barack was a newbie, a shooting star with cool charisma and a Harvard law degree. Like her and Bill, Obama was a brainy "policy wonk," very interested in governmental problem solving, but he had not been tested as she had.

Out to win the Democratic nomination from Senators Clinton and Obama were New Mexico governor Bill Richardson, Ohio congressman Dennis Kucinich, Senators Joe Biden of Delaware and Chris Dodd of Connecticut, and 2004 vice presidential candidate John Edwards, senator from North Carolina. They and the Republican hopefuls thought they'd be effective presidents, but first they had to raise mind-boggling piles of that which fuels politics, American-style: cash. Hillary truly disliked asking people for money. Mostly it came by way of campaign fund-raisers and PACs, political action committees.

## PACs Facts

Often corporations and other organizations want to raise and spend money to affect an election. They form political action committees, to which their people can donate money. The Congress of Industrial Organizations, a trade union, formed the first PAC in 1944, to help reelect President Franklin D. Roosevelt.

As campaigns became ever more costly, Congress formed the Federal Election Commission (FEC) in 1975. This agency makes complicated rules for how campaigns can (and cannot) be paid for—with PACs, for instance. Politicians formed them too, such as Hillary's HillPAC or Obama's Hope Fund, to fund their own and other candidates' campaigns, maybe a promising new politician or one in danger of being voted out of office. Such PACs are useful tools for raising money and support.

To make her radio, TV, and online ads, Hillary chose Mandy Grunwald, Bill's media consultant in 1992, and others, who'd take charge of communications, strategy, and otherwise manage her campaign. Unfortunately, as smart and experienced as her advisers were, they did not work well as a team, and their boss was slow to settle their many disagreements.

Hillary was certain that her staff had what it took to help her win the election. After all, she was the Democrats' leading candidate, their front-runner in the long contest for the presidency. Then President Hillary Clinton would end the wars in Afghanistan and Iraq. She'd tackle America's need for energy independence and do her best to restore the US economy to good health. In George W. Bush's years of waging his expensive War on Terror, Bill Clinton's budget surplus had been pushed back into deficit territory.

First, Candidate Hillary wanted a win in Iowa, the election season's first voting opportunity, a chance to show America that she was the most likely to succeed. So Bill and Chelsea accompanied Hillary on a nine-day "Big Challenges, Real Solutions: Time to Pick a President" tour through the state.

Meanwhile, Obama grew even more popular, thanks to the support of influential TV queen Oprah Winfrey. On January 3, 2008, when it came time to vote, 239,000 Iowans (nearly twice the turnout four years earlier) left their warm homes for church basements and high school gyms to have their say. Hillary came in third, behind handsome John Edwards, whose campaign would quickly fizzle out, and the winner, Barack Obama. Hillary was stunned. Her campaign had poured millions of dollars into Iowa. How could this have happened? Bill grumbled that Obama must have cheated, bused in supporters from Illinois.

"Maybe," Hillary murmured, "they just don't like me."

The question came up, in fact, two days later at the candidates' debate in New Hampshire. Its important primary was coming up on January 8. What would Hillary say, one of the moderators wondered, to the voters who seemed to like Senator Obama more?

"Well, that hurts my feelings," Hillary replied, smiling. "But I'll try to go on . . . I don't think I'm that bad."

Without looking up from his notes, Obama offered a casual, "You're likable enough, Hillary."

She politely thanked him, but his offhand manner stung. Hillary felt that if she'd spoken to Obama like that, she'd be criticized for rudeness. Wouldn't she seem harsh if she played hardball politics with a man who might be the first African-American president? Neither she nor her argumentative team could decide how to approach her much-admired opponent—or how Hillary should present herself, possibly the country's first *woman* president. But just as Obama downplayed his race, Hillary didn't want to call attention to her gender, lest voters think she wasn't tough and serious enough for the job.

So, at that debate, Hillary merely pointed out that the important question wasn't about being liked. It was about being experienced enough to be president. She knew *she* was. "Making change is not about what you believe," she declared. "It's not about a speech you make. It is about working hard. . . . I'm not just running on a promise of change. I'm running on thirty-five years of change . . . what we need is somebody who can *deliver* change!"

Still, Hillary was worried. If she followed her Iowa defeat with another in New Hampshire, her campaign would be in dire trouble, but she had to keep trying. So, on the day before the vote, she put on her makeup, a tailored pantsuit, and a smile. About a hundred reporters with cameras and microphones were waiting at a Portsmouth, New Hampshire, café to record her conversation with sixteen undecided voters. When one of the women asked her how she got out the door every day, Hillary paused before answering. To her, the real question was how on earth, when she was under so much pressure, did she keep going?

"I just don't want to see us fall backward as a nation," Hillary replied. "I mean, this is very personal for me. Not just political. . . . Some people think elections are a game: who's up or who's down," she said, her voice breaking. Her eyes glittered with tears. "It's about our country. It's about our kids' future. It's about all of us together. Some of us put ourselves out there and do this against some difficult odds. . . . We do it because we care about our country. Some of us are right, and some of us are not. Some of us are ready, and some of us are not. Some of us know what we will do on day one, and some of us haven't thought that through." Hillary composed herself before continuing, so softly that her sympathetic listeners had to strain to hear her over the clicking camera shutters. "This is one of the most important elections we'll ever face. So," she continued after another pause, "as tired as I am and I *am* tired . . . I just believe . . . so strongly in who we are as a nation. I'm going to do everything I can to make my case, and then the voters get to decide."

They decided on Hillary. She won a New Hampshire comeback every bit as important as Bill's, sixteen years earlier. As a girl, growing up with her harsh father, Hillary had learned to hide her feelings. Her mother taught her to control her emotions and keep them steady. Her parents' lessons helped Hillary manage her career, often-difficult marriage, and the turbulent White House years, but it was a small-but-golden turning point in her presidential quest when she showed her earnest and warmhearted human self. Not that she was happy about it. She knew that everyone would have something to say about her "emotional moment," letting her game face slip. She was right. Critics William Kristol and Maureen Dowd were quick to say that Hillary "pretended to cry" and "played the female victim."

Hillary went on to win the vote counts in Nevada, Michigan, and Florida, but as the historic, emotionally charged election rolled on, a few mini scandals erupted. Some voters thought that Hillary disrespected Dr. Martin Luther King Jr. when she said that "it took a president," Lyndon B. Johnson, to make Dr. King's dream of racial equality come true by passing the 1964 Civil Rights Act. And when she lost the vote in South Carolina (January 26), Bill Clinton compared Obama's victory to that of African-American Jesse Jackson's wins there in 1984 and '88. Was the ex-president suggesting that Obama only won because of his race, thanks to black voters? Was Bill *too* eager for his wife to win—or was he accidentally-on-purpose hurting her chances? Whatever the answer, both Clintons detested the way this campaign season was going—and that was *before* they got their feelings badly hurt: On January 27, Hillary's powerful fellow senator, Edward Kennedy, and his niece Caroline, President Kennedy's daughter, gave their formidable support to Senator Obama. His idealistic speeches were more inspiring than Hillary's "ready on day one" know-how. Still, the less likely her nomination seemed to be, the stronger Hillary grew as a confident candidate and the more determined she was to fight to the bitter end.

Senator Obama, with his cool, compelling way of speaking, captured the attention of African-American, younger, and more educated citizens. Hillary's voters tended to be older, white, working-class people, and, of course, women. Many, like Hillary's mother, had been born before women were even *allowed* to vote. Hillary inspired their devotion along with victories in the big states of New York and California. She won twenty-one other races in that long, mean election season, including the South Dakota primary, June 3. But that was the day Obama won Montana, when his delegate count went past 2,117, enough to secure the Democratic presidential nomination. It was close. Both he and Hillary had won about eighteen million votes, but she'd lost the race.

It would be 2013 before Hillary Clinton paid off her $12 million campaign debt. By then, she'd feel better about the man who defeated her. But for now, she was so tired and sad, angry and disappointed with the voters' decision. It was awful, feeling like she'd let everybody down, including herself. Still, on the following Saturday, at Washington's National Building Museum, Hillary let the crowd hear her forceful call to battle: "[We must] take our energy, our passion, our strength, and do all we can to help elect Barack Obama, the next president of the United States!"

She saluted the suffragists, "who kept fighting until women could cast their votes. . . . the abolitionists who struggled and died to see the end of slavery," and "the civil rights heroes and foot soldiers who marched, protested, and risked their lives to bring about the end of segregation."

She reminded her audience, "As we gather here today in this historic, magnificent building, the fiftieth woman to leave this Earth is orbiting overhead. If we can blast fifty women into space, we will someday launch a woman into the White House. Although we weren't able to shatter that highest, hardest glass ceiling this time, thanks to you, it's got about eighteen million cracks in it . . ."

Again and again, the crowd interrupted Hillary's gallant speech with their cheers and applause. Hillary had to watch the final vote count that November from the sidelines, but at least she got to see Senators Barack Obama and Joe Biden defeat the Republicans, Senator John McCain and his running mate, Alaska governor Sarah Palin. A few days later Hillary received a phone call. Just as Bill Clinton had done sixteen years earlier, President-Elect Barack Obama was planning his Cabinet of advisers, and he had a job in mind for Hillary. Long before she was his fierce, political opponent, Senator Clinton was his smart, tough friend. Mr. Obama offered, asked, and at least three times, she refused. Then she accepted. After all, as Hillary told her supporters, "Every moment wasted looking back keeps us from moving forward."

## CHAPTER 10

# MADAME SECRETARY

**January 21, 2009–February 1, 2013**
Now, this is not just about meeting with leaders.
—Hillary Rodham Clinton, February 15, 2009

ON MONDAY, DECEMBER 1, 2008, AT A PODIUM bristling with microphones, President-Elect Barack Obama told the American people that he'd asked Senator Hillary Clinton, his former political rival, to be his secretary of state. After the long, painful campaign, Hillary had been looking forward to a quieter life. But as she said, "When your president asks you to serve, you should say yes."

## The Secretary of State

The secretary, the highest-ranking Cabinet officer, serves as the president's main foreign policy adviser. He or she heads the US Department of State, part of our government's executive branch. The secretary has custody of the Great Seal of the United

States, used to seal formal treaties and proclamations. Wherever the secretary goes, to visit foreign leaders, to the United Nations or other international gatherings, he or she represents the United States of America.

The State Department manages US diplomacy, the art and science of dealing with others effectively, with sensitivity and knowledge of other people's and nations' history—where they're coming from, so to speak. Because America is so powerful, it is often drawn in to settle nations' thorny difficulties with one another, such as those between the Palestinians and the Israelis or between North Korea and its neighbors.

Secretaries of state such as James Madison worked with President Jefferson, negotiating the Louisiana Purchase from France. George C. Marshall, in President Truman's administration, helped Europe to recover after World War II. President Clinton appointed the first woman to head the State Department, Madeleine Albright, in 1996. His successor, George W. Bush, chose the first African Americans to occupy this lofty, serious post: General Colin Powell, then Condoleezza Rice.

President Obama and his team faced a tall task. The US economy needed boosting after the giant, scary banking crisis that exploded as George W. Bush's presidency was ending. And as the world's people noted the long, deadly wars in Iraq and Afghanistan, many had formed negative feelings about the United States. It would be Secretary Clinton's job to help rebuild America's international reputation, its brand. She meant to patch up its friendships with other nations and promote American business, as well as improve life for the world's women and girls.

Her many adventures had taught her much, but now Hillary devoured thick State Department briefing books, loaded with a world's worth of in-depth background information. She sought advice from former secretaries, such as "Condi" Rice and Madeleine Albright, Hillary's longtime friend and mentor. She had to be prepared for her job interview at the Senate. It has a Constitutional duty to advise and consent to the president's choices for high-level government positions. So, as the cameras whirred and clicked, Hillary's fellow senators spent several days questioning her before voting (94–2) to confirm her nomination on January 21, 2009. It was Hillary's last day as Senator Clinton. That evening, at the State Department, Bill, Chelsea, and Hillary's mother held Hugh Rodham's small worn Bible as Vice President Joe Biden administered Secretary Clinton's oath of office. The First-Lady-turned-senator was now the sixty-seventh secretary of state. Who had been the first? Thomas Jefferson, in President Washington's Cabinet.

On January 23, Secretary Clinton, dressed in one of her signature pantsuits, climbed into an armored government car, along with her Diplomatic Security agent and her longtime aide, Huma Abedin, now Hillary's deputy chief of staff. (Her staff chief, lawyer Cheryl Mills, had worked in the Clinton White House.) Off they went to Foggy Bottom, where mists and smoke once swirled around Washington's slums and factories on the Potomac's riverfront. Later on, in the 1960s, came the big, slick Kennedy Center for the Performing Arts. And just north of the Lincoln Memorial is the impressively large Harry S. Truman Building, where the US State Department is headquartered. The workers there call it "the Building."

More than a thousand of them waited outside, waving and cheering at the sight of the shiny black car. Hillary climbed out, calling, "Hello! Hello!" Inside, in the grand flag-lined lobby, hundreds more clapped and snapped cell phone photos of their new boss. She greeted them all. "This is going to be a great adventure!"

An elevator whisked Hillary up to her seventh-floor office and wood-paneled study. Down on the second floor, in one of the Building's 4,975 rooms, reporters from major newspapers, TV and radio networks, and international news services were eager to hear what the new secretary had in mind. The main thing was establishing a new, different direction.

As with all new presidencies, President Obama's team was determined to zig where the previous administration had zagged. In her studies, Hillary had embraced a theory that made the most sense to her when it came to doing her new job: smart power—not that former secretaries had practiced dumb power. Managing a huge nation's foreign policy and working the levers of international power and personalities were far more complicated than that. But Hillary agreed with those who felt, for instance, that the war in Iraq might not have gone so tragically out of control if President Bush's team had balanced its invasion with more State Department information about Iraq's complex history and culture. Certainly, most actions had unintended consequences, but Hillary meant to do her best, "choosing the right combination of tools—diplomatic, economic, military, political, legal, and cultural—for each situation."

For now, her schedule was a whirlwind of meetings with the president, the vice president, and the National Security Council. The NSC included Mr. Obama,

Mr. Biden, the secretaries of state, defense, and the treasury, plus the military chairman of the joint chiefs of staff and the assistants for economic policy and national security affairs. They talked over the current international situation, dangers, and where Secretary Clinton should go on her first official trip overseas. Here's a hint:

"We do see Asia as part of America's future," Hillary told the reporters going with her, her assistants, security agents, plus other officials on their weeklong SAM (Special Air Mission) to the Far East. On Sunday, February 15, 2009, a Boeing 757, with the secretary of state's seal fixed to the door, set off from Andrews Air Force Base in Maryland to Tokyo, Japan, 6,781 miles (10,913 km) away. From there, they'd go on to Indonesia, South Korea, and China.

For any such complex diplomatic journey, there is intense preparation. Background information must be gathered. Gifts, formal occasions, itineraries, and talking points are planned, speeches written. Each day's events were carefully detailed and placed in Secretary Clinton's leather notebook. All the while, reporters watched, asked, listened, analyzed, wrote and sent out stories about her travels, meetings with local citizens, activists, business owners, and of course, leaders and foreign ministers.

On this trip, for example, the topic for Hillary's meeting with Japanese officials was the fact that US forces were still in Japan, more than fifty years after the end of World War II. Hillary also met with Emperor Akihito and Empress Michiko, who'd been her and Bill's guests of honor in 1994, in the White House, at their first state dinner.

Next, some 3,500 miles (5,600 km) away in Jakarta, Indonesia's capital on the island of Java, she discussed US relationships with the Southeast Asian nations before her six-hour flight to snowy South Korea. There and in many of her journeys to come, Secretary Clinton spoke of economic issues and empowering women. "People who think hard about our future," she told a mostly female audience, "come to the same conclusion, that women and others on society's margins must be afforded the right to fully participate in society, not only because it is morally right, but because it is necessary to strengthen our security and prosperity."

When she talked with China's leaders, Secretary Clinton would not upset them as she had in 1995, equating women's rights with human rights. (Though she did make time to meet with Chinese women's rights activists.) Nor would she mention the government's harsh treatment of some Chinese citizens. This upset some of her critics, but Hillary was speaking for the United States, not herself. It was her duty to smooth relations between America and its biggest trading partner, China. It is the world's second-biggest economy, and not incidentally, the United States owes China a great deal of money. After a week of traveling, fifteen speeches, eleven media interviews, seven press conferences, and six town hall gatherings, Hillary's team flew home.

During her four years as secretary, Hillary kept up this breathless pace, going 956,733 miles to and from 112 countries. In between, she had the busy happiness of Chelsea's wedding, on July 31, 2010, to Marc Mezvinsky, a young investment banker. She weathered sorrow, with the death of her good friend Richard Holbrooke, the ace diplomat who'd been trying to smooth America's often thorny dealings with Afghanistan and Pakistan.

Wanting the State Department to have a stronger role in the nation's security, Hillary worked closely with Defense Secretary Robert Gates. She worked hard, soothing the feelings of foreign leaders, after WikiLeaks, a journalistic organization that shares information not meant to be published, released *un*diplomatic "private" communications sent between some of the more than 270 US embassies and consulates around the world. Along the way, photographers caught images of the globe-traveling secretary, with her long hair swept back with a headband or scrunchie, e-mailing and texting colleagues on her smartphone throughout her eighteen-hour-a-day schedule. Hillary encouraged her ambassadors' use of Twitter and Facebook, to take part in the international conversation. (Only much later would she have to defend the security of her digital communications.)

In Hillary's four years at State, 2011 stands out for a fateful decision she made and the violent ends of two very different, dreadful leaders. One death closed a chapter. The other led to a complex tragedy that still haunts her. She would meet one personal heroine and lose another, the one dearest to her heart.

In April 2011, Secretary Clinton sent her friend J. Christopher "Chris" Stevens, a dedicated, Arabic-speaking diplomat, to serve in Libya, in North Africa. Just weeks later, Hillary was in the White House Situation Room, with the president and the rest of his National Security team. All were tense, all eyes on a screen full of a dangerous second-by-second endgame. For months they'd been discussing what they knew of Osama bin Laden. The man behind the militant organization al-Qaeda and the 9/11 attacks in 2001 had been hiding ever since. Now President Obama had given a very risky order. In the wee black hours of May 2, 2011, twenty-five bold Navy SEALs in two Black Hawk helicopters raided a compound in Pakistan. Gunfire lit up the darkness. Bin Laden, the world's most wanted terrorist, was killed. Before the year ended, a brutal dictator would meet an even more violent end. His troubles began in the Arab Spring.

## The Arab Spring

In January 2011, in the North African nation of Tunisia, a young fruit vendor took his own life. He could no longer put up with the government obstacles and corrupt policemen that kept him from earning his living. His death sparked the Arab Spring, a wave of protests throughout the Arab world against its stern governments. It was as if grass was pushing up, green and hopeful, out from under iron boots. For decades, men such as Syria's Bashar al-Assad, Libya's Muammar al-Qaddafi, and Hosni Mubarak, Egypt's modern-day pharaoh, had ruled harshly to control their lands, which were plagued with old troubles between tribes and religious groups.

The protests led the Tunisian and Egyptian leaders to step down, but al-Assad turned Syria's uprising into an ongoing, ferocious, and deadly civil war. Libya's troubles morphed into fighting between those for and against Qaddafi. In the end, Secretary Clinton encouraged the use of US airstrikes to help Arabs bring down his dictatorship. Libyans celebrated Qaddafi's violent death on October 20, 2011. Hillary happened to be in Libya shortly before his demise. "We came, we saw, he died," she said later, not so very diplomatically.

For now, the world shudders and wonders about the fate of war-torn Syria. What will come of the deadly uprising best known as ISIS, the Islamic State of Iraq and Syria? So far, a violent, scary season seems to have resulted from the hopeful Arab Spring.

Hillary had just returned from a trip to the Central Asian country Uzbekistan when she heard that frail, ninety-two-year-old Dorothy Rodham had been rushed to the hospital. "I sat by her bedside and held her hand one last time. . . . No one had a bigger influence on my life or did more to shape the person I became." Hillary's mother died on November 1, 2011.

A month later, Secretary Clinton was in Southeast Asia, visiting the harsh military rulers of Burma, aka Myanmar. Lately they'd allowed their isolated people a bit more freedom. They'd even released their best-known political prisoner, Aung San Suu Kyi. For years, the slender opposition leader had been under house arrest due to the success of her political party, the National League for Democracy. Now that the government had freed her, perhaps the United States would give Myanmar some aid?

Hillary was there to tell them yes, to encourage them in their reforms, and to meet with Suu Kyi, whom she so admired. In 1991 Suu Kyi was awarded the Nobel Peace Prize for her brave democratic activism. Now, in late 2011, in the old city of Rangoon (aka Yangon), Suu Kyi, sixty-six, and Hillary, sixty-four, sat with their hair up in ponytails, discussing books they'd read and Myanmar's progress. Later on, in April 2012, the Burmese people voted Suu Kyi's party to their parliament by a landslide.

Meanwhile, far to the west, different groups and tribes of Libyans were fighting over control of their country. Some were armed Islamists, who so despised having non-Muslim Westerners in Libya that they fired their weapons at a UN supply convoy, the International Red Cross headquarters, and a US diplomatic outpost in the Libyan city of Benghazi. US Ambassador Chris Stevens was there.

The whole region was already tense on that September 11, 2012, the eleventh anniversary of the 9/11 attacks. Moreover, an amateur anti-Muslim video-gone-viral had infuriated the local populations. Angry Egyptians ripped down the American flag at Cairo's US embassy. That afternoon Secretary Clinton, just returned from a trip to Russia, was told that armed men with rocket-propelled grenades (RPGs) had stormed the walls of the Benghazi compound. They splashed it with diesel fuel and set it afire, filling it with thick, choking, blinding smoke. Then they attacked another building nearby, staffed with CIA (Central Intelligence Agency) security agents.

For the next twelve hours, Hillary was e-mailing, calling, and videoconferencing with officials and foreign leaders, all trying to find out what was happening as it happened. Four Americans were killed, despite the Libyan security forces who tried to save ex-Navy SEALs Tyrone S. Woods and Glen Doherty, US Foreign Service officer Sean Smith, and Ambassador Stevens. Their flag-draped coffins arrived at Andrews Air Force Base three days later. There to meet them were their shocked and grief-shattered friends and families, President Obama, and sorrowful Secretary Clinton. "We will wipe away our tears," she said, "stiffen our spines, and face the future undaunted."

Even as the somber ceremony went on, arguments crackled all over DC and talk radio: What *really* happened in Benghazi? The tragedy led to one of Hillary's most dramatic and memorable moments, just as her term as secretary was ending. (Months before, President Obama had asked her to stay for a second term, but no. For Hillary, one was enough.)

On September 16, Susan Rice, the US Ambassador to the UN, appeared on TV news programs to explain the Benghazi attacks, but at this early date, she had incomplete information. When Secretary Clinton went to Capitol Hill on September 20, she told the lawmakers that Islamic terrorists likely carried out the deadly attack, not necessarily local Muslims protesting the offensive video, as Ambassador Rice suggested.

The questioners pounced, saying Ms. Rice lied, that Hillary wasn't telling the whole truth. They wanted to find the truth, but being politicians, they wouldn't mind making the Obama administration look bad. Election Day was coming: November 6, 2012. Republicans badly wanted their candidate, Mitt Romney, to defeat President Obama.

But the president was reelected, thanks in part to Bill Clinton's dazzler of a speech in Charlotte, North Carolina, at the Democratic National Convention.

In December, Hillary came home sick from a European trip. A nasty stomach bug left her so weakened that she fainted, hit her head, and suffered a concussion. Hillary's doctor ordered her to stay home and rest, rather than answer more questions about Benghazi. Political wisecrackers said that she was faking an illness, a convenient case of "Benghazi flu." So it was a news event when, on January 23, 2013, Secretary Clinton returned to Capitol Hill to testify before Congress about the embassy attack.

Hillary had been hospitalized for a dangerous blood clot on her brain. Now photographers swarmed her, eager to catch close-ups of her new glasses. A patterned film on the left lens corrected the double vision caused by her injury. Adding to the buzz was the fact that now, at the end of her term, Secretary Clinton had released an official report on the Benghazi catastrophe. In it, she took official responsibility for what had happened on her watch. Actions were listed that would prevent another such attack. Because of the security breakdowns that led to the tragedy, four State Department employees lost their jobs. Secretary Clinton seated herself before the Senate Foreign Relations Committee. Its chairman, Massachusetts senator John Kerry, soon would be the next secretary of state.

Hillary's voice broke as she told about hugging the loved ones of the men who'd died. One by one, the senators thanked her for her service before launching into their statements and questions. Ron Johnson, Wisconsin's Republican senator, began with Ms. Rice's "misleading the American public" on purpose on those news programs. His questioning quickly grew so heated that Secretary Clinton lost her temper.

"With all due respect," Hillary said, her voice rising, "the fact is we had *four dead Americans*! Was it because of a protest? Or was it because of guys out for a walk one night who decided they'd go kill some Americans? What difference at this point does it make?" she demanded impatiently. "It is our job to figure out what happened and do everything we can to prevent it from ever happening again . . . the fact is that people were trying in real time to get to the best information."

Later, Republican senator Rand Paul, from Kentucky, confronted Secretary Clinton with his observation.

"Ultimately, with your leaving, you accept the culpability [guilt] for the worst tragedy since 9/11. . . . Had I been president at the time, and I found that you did not read the cables from Benghazi . . . I would have relieved you of your post. I think it's inexcusable."

Despite the senator's sharp words, Hillary knew well that, of the many thousands of worldwide messages constantly flooding into the State Department, it was impossible for employees to know which ones *had to* get to the top executive immediately. Still, the tragedy at Benghazi would remain her most sorrowful regret from her years as secretary of state, which ended February 1, 2013.

Far-traveling Secretary Clinton had employed a great deal of face-to-face diplomacy to raise America's standing in the world and champion people's economic issues, public health, and an Internet where ideas are freely shared. She even created a new diplomatic position: an ambassador-at-large specifically for global women's issues. To publicly thank Hillary for her service, President Obama invited her to be with him on *60 Minutes*—twenty-one years after her first appearance on the CBS program. Then, she and Bill were trying to save their 1992 campaign. Now the same interviewer, Steve Kroft, wanted to know how Hillary and

Mr. Obama went from political enemies to strong friends.

"Part of our bond is we've been through a lot of the same stuff," said the president. "Getting whacked around in political campaigns, being criticized in the press. You know, we've both built some pretty thick skins."

They had. But was Hillary willing to get "whacked" around in one more race for the presidential prize? She'd be asked that a lot. That much about the future Hillary knew for sure.

## CHAPTER 11

# THE CHAMPION

**February 2, 2013–Present**
Wife, mom, lawyer, women & kids advocate, FLOAR,
FLOTUS, US Senator, SecState, author, dog owner, hair icon,
pantsuit aficionado, glass ceiling cracker, TBD . . .
—Twitter @HillaryClinton, June 10, 2013

They throw all this stuff at me and I'm still standing.
—Hillary Rodham Clinton, Des Moines, Iowa, January 25, 2016

FROM 1980 TO 1991, HILLARY RODHAM CLINTON balanced lawyering and motherhood with her service as FLOAR (First Lady of Arkansas), before setting out on that killer cross-country 1992 presidential campaign. Then came eight difficult years on the White House scandal roller coaster. Hillary followed all that with a Senate campaign, her service on Capitol Hill, and a rough, tough battle for her party's presidential nomination, all before setting out on her nonstop, four-year stint as secretary of state! No wonder Hillary joked about filling her life's next chapter with little more than "beaches . . . speeches."

Not quite.

Sure, after the past relentless years, Hillary relished the simple pleasure of strolling along Long Island's seashore with Bill and their white poodle and chocolate Lab. She enjoyed reading detective novels instead of briefing books and sleeping in a bit later than usual, after staying up late watching *House of Cards*. She and Bill loved the Netflix miniseries about fictional political wheeler-dealers—while remaining usefully occupied in the real world, in the public eye.

Hillary signed up with an agency that set up high-paying speaking gigs for its important clients, such as Bono, Barbara Walters, and Bill Clinton. In the twelve years after leaving office, the former president delivered 542 speeches around the world, earning $105 million. In 2014 and the first three months of 2015, Hillary earned $11 million. Much of this she donated to her family's foundation. Still, for a poor fatherless southern boy and the daughter of frugal Hugh Rodham, theirs was a great deal of money.

Hillary recorded a video statement for LGBT (lesbian, gay, bisexual, and transgender) Americans' civil rights, including gay citizens' right to legally marry their partners. Taking a stand on this controversial issue was a strong political statement in 2013, when the Supreme Court's historic decision for same-sex marriage, nationwide, was more than two years away. Presidential politics-watchers wondered if Hillary Clinton *had* decided to make another run for the White House. Whenever asked, though, her answer was no. Still, loyal Hillarylanders had their Ready for Hillary super PAC up and going, gathering names of supporters and donors, just in case.

Hillary checked another thing off her spring 2013 to-do list when she launched her Twitter account—and scored more than 360,000 followers in the first twenty-four hours. She linked up with her husband's foundation too.

## The Clinton Foundation

In 1997 President Clinton started his foundation as a way to make his post–White House dreams come true: a presidential library and museum in Little Rock and a graduate school of public service at the University of Arkansas. Bill accomplished these after he left office, and a variety of international charity projects, through the Clinton Foundation. It was a nongovernmental organization (NGO) that could bring together individuals, governments, and other NGOs to help people. Nelson Mandela of South Africa helped to inspire one of its first programs, to connect HIV/AIDS sufferers with care and medicine.

In 2005 Doug Band, Clinton's assistant since his presidential days, saw a way to turn his boss's fame, personality, brains, and many interests into the Clinton Global Initiative. Once a year, the ex-president could bring together scholars, Nobel Prize winners, leaders of nations, corporations, foundations, NGOs, billionaires, and superstars to brainstorm fresh ways to fix the world's thorny problems and drum up substantial donations to finance their solutions.

When some of Mr. Band's methods sparked controversy, Chelsea Clinton joined the family business. The Bill, Hillary, and Chelsea Clinton Foundation, as it's been known since 2013, is a collection of programs devoted to such issues as energy, climate change, access to clean water, and helping people overcome poverty, ignorance, and disease. All of these affect the lives of women and children, but Hillary Clinton launched special programs just for their empowerment, as she'd done for many years. If the Clintons' bright constellation of good works cast any shadow, it was in the form of questions about how properly the foundation accounted for the great sums of money it handled, some donated by foreign governments— questions that the ex–secretary of state could face if she braved the campaign trail once more.

In addition to everything else going on in her life, Hillary had a multimillion-dollar book contract. With a trio of research assistants (Hillary's "book team"), she wrote *Hard Choices*, about her international diplomatic adventures. When it was published in June 2014, every important interviewer invited Hillary to come talk about her book and about her first grandchild, due in the fall. But most of all, they asked Hillary what she'd asked herself in her book: "Will I run for president in 2016? The answer is, I haven't decided yet."

Hillary always liked—no, she *needed* to mull things over. She absolutely knew that running for president was, in her words, a "very combative, even brutal experience." Everyone would question and comment on her life, her family, their work, her face, and everything she wore or said. Why on earth would she tackle it again?

At her core, Hillary Clinton was a determined do-gooder, a public servant. As an artist uses paint or clay, her medium was government; and if a difficult, expensive campaign was what it cost to perform high-profile public service, Hillary had the ambition and backbone to pay the price. She also had the joy of her family, of being with Bill, of delighting in their new baby granddaughter, Charlotte Clinton Mezvinsky, born September 26, 2014.

# Chelsea Clinton

By autumn 2014, the former First Daughter with the braces and wild mane of curls was a thirty-four-year-old wife, mother, and businesswoman. After earning a history degree at Stanford, where she met her future husband, Marc Mezvinsky, Chelsea Clinton continued her studies in England. Like her dad, she went to Oxford University, where she earned master's and doctorate degrees in international relations. She took extra studies in public health and settled in New York City in 2004, with a crisp new job as a business consultant.

Chelsea worked on her mother's 2008 campaign, then at an investment firm. For all her brilliance and education, there were those who said that Chelsea earned a lot, not for what she did, but for who she was, especially in the years 2011–2014, when NBC News paid her a yearly $600,000 to be a "special correspondent."

Then, in 2013, Chelsea became vice chair of her family's foundation.

"While I was on Wall Street, I realized that the things I was most passionate about were the things my parents were most passionate about," she said. To encourage young people to take an active part in improving their world, Chelsea wrote a book, published in the fall of 2015: *It's Your World: Get Informed, Get Inspired & Get Going!*

In March 2015 Hillary was still pondering a presidential run and the lessons she'd learned from the 2008 campaign, when her actions as secretary of state inspired headline news: she had done all her personal—and official—messaging by way of her private e-mail account. "Looking back," said Hillary, in her own defense, "it would have been better for me to use two separate phones and two e-mail accounts. I thought using one device would be simpler, and obviously, it hasn't worked out that way."

True, Hillary had gone by the regulations in place at the time. Stricter rules came about after she left State. She maintained that she didn't send or receive any top secret information, but some documents were reclassified later on. (Officials often argue over what should be a government secret.) But the storm around Hillary grew stormier when it turned out that her e-mails had been routed through a private server at her home in Chappaqua, New York. The former secretary of state lived there with ex-President Clinton so Secret Service people guarded their house from burglars or would-be assassins. But the possibility of computer viruses or hackers getting into the communications of a senior Cabinet officer—this was a very different matter.

Hillary turned over about half of her messages, some 55,000 e-mails, which, at this writing, intelligence officers in the State Department and elsewhere in the government continue to examine. Now, as in the nerve-racking Whitewater scandal, Hillary's critics questioned her judgment. Still, she certainly was not someone to let controversy keep her from deciding to do what she thought was right for herself, and for the public good, no matter how difficult.

Hillary knew from hard experience what any presidential candidate must endure, just for the chance to lead the troubled American people. The citizens, their news sources, and lawmakers were still divided, despite Barack Obama's hopeful, soaring words in 2004 about bringing the country together. The wide gap between the wealthy few and everyone else made the American dream feel far less possible, less equally shared.

Whoever managed to become the forty-fifth American president on Inauguration Day, January 20, 2017, would face complex challenges: Helping the aging US population adapt to changes in their schools and jobs, to keep up with advancing information technology and the ever-changing world economy. Responding to citizens protesting, under the banner of Black Lives Matter, the unfairness in America's system of law and order. Leading a people who don't trust their gridlocked government's ability to fix things—the country's crumbling network of roads, bridges, and water pipes, for example. Commanding the US Armed Forces in a warming, crowded world full of struggling nations, producing refugees, immigrants, extremists, frustration, and fear.

Who'd want this, the toughest job in the world? Hillary did. Like many a man who'd gone before, she believed in her ability to make her mark on history. On Sunday afternoon, April 12, 2015, in her announcement video, the vast voting public saw and heard her smile and say, "I'm running for president!"

"Americans have fought their way back from tough economic times," she continued. "But the deck is still stacked in favor of those at the top. Everyday Americans need a champion, and I want to be that champion so you can do more than just get by. You can get ahead and stay ahead. Because when families are strong, America is strong. So I'm hitting the road to earn your vote, because it's your time. And I hope you'll join me on this journey."

It promised to be a bumpy one. Hopeful candidates would fall away, one by one, as each failed to capture voters' enthusiasm, as America's long, winnowing-out, president-electing process is meant to do. Among the many would-be presidents, former governors Rick Perry (R–TX) and Lincoln Chafee (D–RI) dropped out early on, as did Senator Lindsey Graham (R–SC). Later on, Hillary Clinton would find herself debating former governor Martin O'Malley (D–MD) and Senator Bernie Sanders, the self-proclaimed Democratic Socialist from Vermont. Because of his liberal views, few had high expectations for Bernie's political success—at first.

On Saturday, June 13, 2015, Hillary donned a bright blue pantsuit and set out for Roosevelt Island in Manhattan's East River. Security and media people waited there with the crowd for the rally that would kick off Hillary's official (and likely her last) campaign. Her supporters carried signs with her capital *H* logo: two blue uprights, linked with a bright red arrow. They cheered, *"Hill-a-ry! Hill-a-ry!"*

She talked to them about the American dream. "America's basic bargain: If you do your part you ought to be able to get ahead. . . . That bargain inspired generations of families, including my own."

She spoke of her grandpa and her dad, who worked hard to make their families' lives better, and of modern Americans, not getting ahead no matter how hard they worked. If they gave her the chance, she'd make the economy work for them.

"I believe that success isn't measured by how much the wealthiest Americans have, but by how many children climb out of poverty."

She told the crowd about her mom, who never let her back down from any bully or barrier. And "an America where a father can tell his daughter: yes, you can be anything you want to be, even president of the United States.

"We Americans may differ, bicker, stumble, and fall," she said, "but we are at our best when we pick each other up, when we have each other's back. It's no secret that we're going up against some pretty powerful forces that will do and spend whatever it takes to advance a very different vision for America. But," she declared, "I've spent my life fighting for children, families, and our country. And I'm not stopping now."

The next day, Candidate Clinton was on the road, with Secret Service agents at the wheels of two black vans named *Scooby*. Why? The vans reminded Hillary of one featured in *Scooby-Doo*, the 1970s TV cartoon show. By Monday, she was a thousand miles to the west, talking to and shaking hands with Iowans. Like every other presidential candidate, Hillary urged them to show up on February 1, 2016, and declare their support for her at their caucuses.

## The Iowa Caucuses

Ten states and three US territories hold caucuses. In each of Iowa's 1,681 precincts, citizens brave a winter night to go out to schools, libraries, and other meeting places. At their caucus meetings, Republicans cast secret ballots for their candidate. Democrats, on the other hand, persuade their neighbors to form groups, according to whom they support, to be counted. Either way, the people's choices eventually determine which candidate's delegates go to the political parties' national conventions.

In Cleveland, Ohio, from July 18 to 21, 2016, the Republicans would officially nominate the candidate with a majority of some 2,472 delegates. At the Democrats' convention in Philadelphia, Pennsylvania, July 25–28, the winner of 2,383 delegates' votes (a majority of 4,764) would win the nomination. Some states and territories combine caucuses and primaries, the more common format, where voters simply vote.

The Iowa caucuses gained national importance in 1972, when Democrats scheduled theirs before New Hampshire's primary. That made Iowa's event first in the US election calendar, the voters' first official say. A win there makes a candidate look much

more vote-worthy and electable. That said, in 1992
Bill Clinton did poorly in Iowa, but he went on to win
the White House.

Hillary was disappointed with her 2008 third-place finish in Iowa, proof that she hadn't inspired the kind of
excitement that Barack Obama attracted that year. With
her focus on solving complex problems little by little,
plus all her high-paying speechmaking, on top of her
many—sometimes controversial—years in the public eye,
voters tended to see her as part of the status quo: the
usual way the US government, banks, and corporations
ran modern America. This was the gigantic trio that had
so many citizens feeling ignored and angry. In 2008 they
turned to Obama, who gave lofty talks about hope and
change. Now, seven years later, Americans' mood had not
improved, and Hillary faced another strong, idealistic
contender in the race for the presidential nomination.
This one called for shaking up the establishment, for a
political revolution. Vermont senator Bernie Sanders
wasn't a new face, as Senator Obama had been, in 2008.
At seventy-four, Bernie wasn't young and he was no out-
sider. He'd been in Congress since 1991, but his forceful
socialist views were uncommon in mainstream politics.

He believed that in exchange for more tax dollars, the US government could and *should* improve people's lives by taking charge of their health care, for instance. That made Bernie much more liberal, or progressive, than practical Hillary. She'd set aside liberal views of her own in order to get done what she could; for example, when she tried to reform US health care. Hillary knew from hard experience that it really would take a political revolution for Bernie's agenda to get past all the politicians and deep-pocketed business lobbyists in the US Congress. Wasn't it more important to accomplish progressive change as best she could, within that status quo?

On June 16, 2015, just three days after Hillary launched her campaign, a Republican like none other began his and changed the presidential race. New York City real estate developer and reality TV personality Donald J. Trump was certain that he could, in the words of his slogan, "Make America Great Again." The billionaire celebrity with the distinctive hairdo could be brash, boastful, and rude. He made unlikely promises—and quickly showed his genius at attracting media attention and enormous crowds.

Trump's boldness had the effect of making the other GOP contenders look tame by comparison, even archconservative senator Ted Cruz (R-TX). Candidates such as Senator Marco Rubio (R-FL), former Florida governor John Ellis "Jeb" Bush (loyal son and brother of ex-presidents Bush); and Carly Fiorina, former corporate executive (the sole Republican woman would-be president), all struggled to be taken seriously.

In the midst of all the questing for the future, Hillary had to deal with the past. On October 22, 2015, Republicans in the House of Representatives insisted that she talk with them about the attacks on Benghazi. Hillary showed her heart and stamina over eleven hours of harsh questioning. Two days later Bill Clinton showed his admiration for her, telling a crowd of Iowans that his wife was the person "most likely to keep big, bad things from happening and to make more good things happen." And by the way, wouldn't they please help him by breaking "the stranglehold that women have had on the job of presidential spouse"?

As 2015 ground to an end, Hillary and the other contenders traveled Iowa, making speeches. Journalists filed stories. Fund-raisers begged for contributions. Pundits pondered and organizers organized. Supporters Tweeted, championed their candidates on Facebook, sent mailings, and with the turn of the year, they telephoned voters. The caucuses were at hand. The 2016 election had become a loud American argument: What should their nation be? Could serious, capable Hillary triumph over all the noise? Could she tap into the good history of what she—and Bill—had accomplished? Could she *make* history by becoming Madame President, America's first? The only way to find out was for Hillary to soldier on, smile, listen, answer, and speak her piece until, at last, it was time for voters to have their say in Iowa.

180,000 Republicans and 171,000 Democrats came to the caucuses, not quite 12 percent of Iowa's population. It was a good turnout, considering Americans' glum view of politics and the snowstorm bearing down on the Hawkeye State. Not until two thirty the next morning were the votes completely counted, but late on the night of February 1, 2016, it appeared that Senator Cruz had trumped Donald Trump and Hillary Clinton had pulled off a squeaker. If only by a hair, she edged past Bernie Sanders to a first-place finish.

Bill Clinton stood beside his daughter, Chelsea, who was expecting her second baby later in the campaign summer. Smiling, waving at the crowd, they beamed at bright-red-clad Hillary.

"I stand here tonight, breathing a big sigh of relief," she said, before exclaiming, *"Thank you, IOWA!"*

Election Day was some nine hard months away, but she was geared for the long battle. However it ended, it was clear that Hillary Rodham Clinton's journey would continue. As she told her happy supporters, "I will keep on doing what I have done my entire life."

Soon all three Clintons would be out in the winter night, continuing on.

# HILLARY

ON THAT SUNNY DAY ON ROOSEVELT ISLAND AT THE start of her campaign, Hillary told the crowd that "the story of America is a story of hard-fought, hard-won progress. And it continues today." As does her remarkable story— and may it long continue. For a biographer, individuals who came to their mortal conclusions a while back have an advantage over her. There's been time to fully consider their importance, their places in history. Even as I finish this book, my subject *and* her campaign are still soldiering onward.

Still, I'm just a few years younger than fellow baby boomer Hillary Clinton. So while I researched to get a tighter grip on the times in which she's lived her life, I have memories of my own to draw upon. Besides anxious late-night talks about the war in Vietnam and getting my first copy of *Ms.* magazine, a day in 1992 comes to mind. I went to where Candidate Clinton's wife, wearing her trademark headband, was conducting a Q&A. Not knowing I'd be writing this book one day, I asked her something about her husband's stance on the line item veto—when I might have asked about her post-Wellesley summer of '69. *What kind of car did you drive, Ms. Clinton, when you worked your way across Alaska? Young readers will want to know.* I'll *want to know!*

Not knowing any more in 1992 than I do now about the future, I couldn't warn her about her troubles ahead. And who knew then how important she was going to be, the strong feelings she would inspire, and all that she would come to represent?

For one thing, Hillary is but the latest chapter in a long, long story that began in the summer of 1848, at the first women's rights convention. It's just as well that those angry, determined Victorian ladies in Seneca Falls, New York, couldn't know how long it would take to pry the vote out of the fist of power. Stunned those women would be, at the idea (*and* the pantsuit!) of a future US female with a real, fighting chance to win the presidency. They'd be outraged, but not surprised, that even in the twenty-first century an educated, experienced citizen would *still* have to worry about her face, her hair, looking either too weak or too calculating if she wept in public, not to mention too darned ambitious.

"I challenge assumptions about women," said Hillary in 2009. "I do make some people uncomfortable, which I'm well aware of, but that's just part of coming to grips with what I believe is still one of the most important pieces of unfinished business in human history—empowering women to be able to stand up for themselves."

And that she has tried to do, specifically as US secretary of state, when she made the status of the world's women a central issue in American foreign policy. But Hillary and the criticism she attracts also represent the way public citizenship has been affected by too-divided politics, too-divided sources of 24-7 news, plus billions of dollars. Voters might wonder, what does she still believe? Who is the real Hillary?

"I wonder who is *me*," Hillary wrote, as a college student in 1968. "I wonder if I'll ever meet her. If I did, I think we'd get along famously."

Perhaps. After all, Hillary Diane Rodham Clinton is a

strong, complicated woman in a complicated, dangerous world. One might well imagine, in, as Bill once said, "a place called hope," that there still lives in her heart the girl devoted to doing good, by all the means and in all the ways she ever can.

# ACKNOWLEDGMENTS

IT WAS FALL 2014 WHEN A MESSAGE APPEARED IN my e-mailbox. Would I be interested in writing a Hillary Clinton biography for young readers? With that thrilling e-mail from editor Karen Nagel, followed by our jolly, informative telephone conversation, I was launched on a downright educational adventure. It began with many visits to my local knowledge repository, the North Independence (Missouri) branch of the Mid-Continent Public Library, more than one phone call to its corps of fine research librarians, bless them, and many, *many* hours reading the books I found there.

There followed a drive down to Arkansas, where I had the pleasure of visiting with cheerful, knowledgeable Kate Johnson. She directs the Clinton House Museum, which once was the small brick home, in Fayetteville, of newly-weds Hillary Rodham and Bill Clinton. I thank her for her encouragement and hospitality. Thanks also to Herbert Ragan and John Keller of the William J. Clinton Presidential Library, for their help in sourcing this book's photographs.

# ACKNOWLEDGMENTS

Thank you to my dear agent Susan Schulman. Most especially, thanks and blessings to my indispensable listeners and advisers, Laura Sturman, Vicki Grove, and Veda Boyd Jones, the Voice of Reason. This book is dedicated to them.

# TIME LINE

**October 26, 1947:** Hillary Diane Rodham is born in Chicago, Illinois.

**April 15, 1962:** Hillary hears and meets Reverend Dr. Martin Luther King Jr., speaking in Chicago.

**November 22, 1963:** President John F. Kennedy is assassinated.

**June 9, 1965:** Hillary graduates from Maine South High School, Park Ridge, Illinois.

**1966:** Indira Gandhi becomes prime minister of India.

**April 4, 1968:** Dr. Martin Luther King Jr. is assassinated.

**June 6, 1968:** Robert F. Kennedy is assassinated.

**1968:** Hillary leaves the Republican Party for the Democrats.

**1969:** Golda Meir becomes prime minister of Israel.

**1969:** Hillary receives a BA degree in political science, then addresses fellow graduates of Wellesley College.

**1974:** Hillary receives a doctorate of law from Yale University.

**Spring 1974:** Hillary serves on the advisory staff of the House of Representatives' Judiciary Committee, regarding the impeachment of President Richard M. Nixon.

**August 9, 1974:** President Nixon resigns his office.

**October 11, 1975:** Hillary Rodham and Bill Clinton are married in Fayetteville, Arkansas.

# TIME LINE

**1979:** Margaret Thatcher becomes prime minister of the United Kingdom of Great Britain.

Dr. Maria de Lourdes Pintasilgo is the first woman to serve as Portugal's prime minister.

**January 9, 1979–January 19, 1981:** Bill Clinton serves as fortieth governor of Arkansas.

**1980:** Vigdís Finnbogadóttir becomes president of Iceland, the world's first woman to be elected head of state in a national election.

**February 27, 1980:** Chelsea Victoria Clinton is born.

**January 11, 1983–December 12, 1992:** Bill Clinton serves as forty-second Arkansas governor.

**January 20, 1993:** Bill Clinton becomes forty-second US president. Hillary is First Lady.

**1997:** Hillary receives a Grammy Award for her reading of the recorded version of her 1996 book, *It Takes a Village*.

**January 3, 2001:** First Lady Hillary Clinton is sworn in as New York's junior senator.

**September 11, 2001:** Islamic extremists attack World Trade Center, New York City, and the Pentagon, Washington, DC.

**January 16, 2006:** Ellen Johnson Sirleaf of Liberia becomes Africa's first elected female head of state.

**January 20, 2007:** Hillary launches her presidential campaign.

**January 20, 2009:** Barack Obama is inaugurated as the forty-fourth US president, the first of African descent.

**2009–2013:** Hillary is the sixty-seventh US secretary of state.

**September 11, 2012:** Attack on US diplomatic compound at Benghazi, Libya.

**September 26, 2014:** Chelsea Clinton and husband Marc Mezvinsky welcome their daughter, Charlotte Clinton Mezvinsky, into the world.

**April 12, 2015:** Hillary launches her second run for the presidency.

**June 10, 2015:** Hillary kicks off her campaign at Roosevelt Island, New York City.

**February 1, 2016:** Hillary comes in just barely ahead of Senator Bernie Sanders at the Iowa caucuses, eight days before he defeats her at the New Hampshire Primary.

**February 27, 2016:** At the Democratic Presidential Preference Primary in South Carolina, Hillary has a resounding victory over Senator Sanders, with many a contest still to come before Election Day, November 8, 2016.

## KEY EVENTS DURING
## BILL CLINTON'S PRESIDENCY

## 1993

**February 26.** New York City. A deadly bomb explodes at the World Trade Center.

**February 28–April 19.** Waco, Texas. Suspecting illegal weapons, US agents surround the Branch Davidian compound, home of families devoted to David Koresh, a self-styled Christian prophet. A fifty-one-day siege ends with tear gas and deadly flames.

# TIME LINE

**April–May.** Rwanda. The Hutu people kill nearly 800,000 of their Tutsi countrymen.

**August 10.** Ruth Bader Ginsburg becomes the second female justice on the Supreme Court.

**September 13.** President Clinton brings Israel's Yitzhak Rabin and Palestinian Yasir Arafat together in Washington, DC, to sign a Palestinian self-government agreement.

**October 3.** Mogadishu, Somalia. Bill Clinton sends US Special Forces to capture warlord Mohammed Farah Aidid. Two Black Hawk helicopters are shot down. Eighteen US soldiers are killed, and American troops are ordered out of Somalia.

**December 8.** To promote free trade between the United States, Canada, and Mexico, Clinton signs the North American Free Trade Agreement (NAFTA).

## 1994

**July 25.** President Clinton helps bring about an Israel/Jordan peace agreement.

**September.** Bill Clinton sends troops to Haiti to help democratically elected President Jean Bertrand Aristide take office.

## 1995

**April 19.** Oklahoma City, Oklahoma. US terrorists use a truck bomb to blow up the Alfred P. Murrah Federal Building, killing 168 people.

**July 11.** The United States offers Vietnam full diplomatic recognition.

**November 21.** Dayton, Ohio. With the help of US Ambassador Richard Holbrooke, representatives of Serbia, Croatia, and Bosnia agree to end three years of savage war. President Clinton sends 20,000 US troops to enforce the cease-fire.

# TIME LINE

## 1996

**December 5.** President Clinton appoints UN Ambassador Madeleine Albright to be the first female Secretary of State.

## 1997

**April 24.** The United States Senate passes legislation to ratify the Chemical Weapons Convention, an international agreement ending these weapons' production and use.

**June 26.** J. K. Rowling's first Harry Potter book is published in London.

**August 31.** Diana, Princess of Wales, dies as a res of a Paris car crash.

## 1998

**August 7.** Terrorists, thought to be led by Osa Laden, bomb US embassies in Kenya and T killing 224 people, including twelve Americ

**August 20.** In response, President Clin missile strikes on Afghanistan and Sudar

**December.** Hillary Clinton makes the c

**December 16.** When Iraqi dictator S wouldn't go along with UN wear President Clinton orders air strikes

## 1999

**March 24–June 10.** Southwe forces, including US troops, who have been attacking an

**April 20.** Two Columbin in Colorado shoot and k teacher, then themselve

# TIME LINE

## 2000

**March 26.** Vladimir Putin is elected president of Russia.

**November 7.** Hillary Rodham Clinton elected to US Senate. The close presidential election is left to the mostly conservative Supreme Court to decide—that Republican Texas governor George W. Bush has defeated former vice president Al Gore.

# FURTHER READING
# AND VIEWING

## BOOKS BY HILLARY CLINTON

Clinton, Hillary Rodham. *Dear Socks, Dear Buddy: Kids' Letters to the First Pets*. New York: Simon & Schuster, 1998.

————. *Hard Choices*. New York: Simon & Schuster, 2014.

————. *It Takes a Village*. New York: Simon & Schuster, 1996.

————. *Living History*. New York: Simon & Schuster, 2003.

## BOOKS BY OTHERS

Abrams, Dennis. *Hillary Rodham Clinton, Politician*. New York: Chelsea House, 2009.

Davis, Todd. *The New Big Book of U.S. Presidents*. Philadelphia: Running Press, 2013.

Freedman, Russell. *Eleanor Roosevelt: A Life of Discovery*. New York: Clarion Books, 1993.

Harness, Cheryl. *Ghosts of the White House*. New York: Simon & Schuster, 1998.

Krull, Kathleen. *Hillary Rodham Clinton: Dreams Taking Flight*. Illustrated by Amy June Bates. New York: Simon & Schuster, 2008.

Lee, Sally. *William Jefferson Clinton*. North Mankato, MN: Capstone Press, 2014.

Pastan, Amy. *First Ladies*. New York: Dorling Kindersley Publishing, Inc., 2001.

## ON THE WEB

**Hillary Rodham Clinton**

www.whitehouse.gov/1600/first-ladies/hillaryclinton

# FURTHER READING AND VIEWING

At the White House's site you can find bios of all the presidents, first ladies, and vice presidents, plus info about Camp David, the presidential getaway.

www.pbs.org/wgbh/americanexperience/features/biography/clinton-hillary/

At this page, find background biographical info about Hillary as well as the transcript of the segment devoted to her in *Clinton*, the excellent *American Experience* documentary detailing the glorious, tragic story of the forty-second presidency, available through PBS and on YouTube.

**First Ladies**

www.firstladies.org

A fine, comprehensive introduction to all the women who have carried the ceremonial title "First Lady."

**Hillary for America!**

www.hillaryclinton.com

Find out about the candidate and all the ways you can get involved at Hillary's official presidential campaign site.

**Everything You Need to Know About Hillary Rodham Clinton Prior to 2016**

http://politifact.info/everything-you-need-to-know-about-hillary-prior -to-2016/

**The 1960s–70s American Feminist Movement: Breaking Down Barriers for Women**

https://tavaana.org/en/content/1960s-70s-american-feminist-movement -breaking-down-barriers-women

Here's an excellent introduction to a key period in the life of young Hillary Rodham and American society in the twentieth century.

# SOURCES

## BOOKS

Abrams, Dennis. *Hillary Rodham Clinton, Politician*. New York: Chelsea House, 2009.

Allen, Jonathan, and Amie Parnes. *HRC: State Secrets and the Rebirth of Hillary Clinton*. New York: Crown Publishers, 2014.

Bernstein, Carl. *A Woman in Charge*. New York: Random House, 2007.

Clinton, Hillary Rodham. *Hard Choices*. New York: Simon & Schuster, 2014.

———. *Living History*. New York: Simon & Schuster, 2003.

Drew, Elizabeth. *On the Edge*. New York: Simon & Schuster, 1994.

Gerth, Jeff, and Don Van Natta Jr. *Her Way: The Hopes and Ambitions of Hillary Rodham Clinton*. New York: Little, Brown and Co., 2007.

Ghattas, Kim. *The Secretary: A Journey with Hillary Clinton from Beirut to the Heart of American Power*. New York: Times Books, 2013.

Halper, Daniel. *Clinton, Inc.* New York: Broadside Books, 2014.

Harris, Bill. *The First Ladies Fact Book*. New York: Black Dog & Leventhal, 2009.

Heilemann, John, and Mark Halperin. *Game Change: Obama and the Clintons, McCain and Palin, and the Race of a Lifetime*. New York: HarperCollins, 2010.

Mueller, James E. *Tag Teaming the Press: How Bill and Hillary Clinton Work Together to Handle the Media*. Lanham, MD: Rowman & Littlefield Publishers, Inc., 2008.

Sheehy, Gail. *Hillary's Choice*. New York: Ballantine Books, 1999.

Smith, Sally Bedell. *For Love of Politics: Inside the Clinton White House*. New York: Random House, 2007.

# SOURCES

## ARTICLES

Applebaum, Anne. "Just Words." Slate.com, February 2009.

Bates, Karen Grigsby. "Stokely Carmichael, A Philosopher Behind the Black Power Movement." National Public Radio. *Code Switch.* March 10, 2014.

Breslau, Karen. "Hillary Clinton's Emotional Moment." *Newsweek,* January 6, 2008.

Chafe, William H. "When Bill Met Hillary." *Salon,* September 2, 2012.

Dockterman, Eliana. "Clinton: I Never Denied Smoking Pot." *Time,* December 3, 2013.

Elliot, Annabel Fenwick. "Chelsea Clinton Reveals That After Years of Distancing Her Career from Parents Bill and Hillary—She Is Now 'Proud' to Be Following in Their Famous Footsteps." www.dailymail.com, March 12, 2015.

Hagan, Joe. "Hillary in Midair." *New York Magazine,* September 22, 2013.

Mead, Rebecca. "Hillary for President: No Joke." *The New Yorker,* April 14, 2015.

Miller, Mark. "The War Room Drill." *Newsweek, Special Election Issue,* November/December 1992.

Nagourney, Adam. *New York Times,* July 8, 1999.

Newton-Small, Jay. "3 Takeaways from the Hillary Papers." *Time,* February 10, 2014.

Sheehy, Gail. "What Hillary Wants." *Vanity Fair,* May 1992.

Smith, Ben. "Clinton and Obama, Johnson and King." *Politico,* January 7, 2008.

Tumulty, Karen. "The Woman Who Tried to Talk Hillary Out of Marrying Bill." *Time,* January 3, 2008.

# SOURCES

Van Meter, Jonathan. "Her Brilliant Career." *Vogue,* December 2009.

Waldman, Ayelet. "Is This Really Goodbye?" *Marie Claire,* October 18, 2012.

## INTERVIEWS

Laura Brown's interview with HRC. "Hillary Clinton: Myth and Reality." *Harper's Bazaar,* February 14, 2011.

Mark Miller's interview with HRC. "Lessons of a Lightning Rod." *Newsweek, Special Election Issue,* November 1992.

Ed Pilkington's interview with HRC. "Will She or Won't She Run for President in 2016?" *The Guardian,* June 21, 2014.

# SOURCE NOTES

### Epigraph

"Women are the . . . in the world." International Crisis Group "In Pursuit of Peace" Award Dinner, New York City, December 16, 2011.

### Introduction

p. 2: "somebody who . . . going to do it?'" Hagan, *New York Magazine*.

p. 2: "Do all the good . . . as ever you can." John Wesley, quoted in *Living History*, p. 22.

### Chapter 1

p. 3: "I was born an American . . . and place." *Living History*, p. 1.

p. 6: "There's no room . . . for cowards." *Living History*, p. 12.

### Chapter 2

p. 13: "The times they are a-changin'." Lyrics from "The Times They Are A-Changin'," Bob Dylan, 1964.

p. 13: "We arrived . . . possible." Hillary's commencement speech, May 31, 1969.

p. 15: "Wellesley . . . when we left." *Living History*, p. 27.

p. 22: "I can't take it!" Bernstein, *A Woman in Charge*, p. 53.

p. 25: "cheerful, good humored." Wellesley president Ruth M. Adams. Ibid., p. 58.

p. 25: Text of Hillary D. Rodham's student commencement speech. http://www.wellesley.edu/events/commencement/archives/1969commencement/studentspeech.

p. 25: "The Art of Making Possible." Poem by Nancy Scheibner. Ibid.

# SOURCE NOTES

## Chapter 3

p. 27: "You have . . . yourself." Waldman, *Marie Claire*.

p. 28: "Black . . . beautiful." Bates, NPR.

p. 31: "like a Viking . . . hair." *Living History*, p. 52.

p. 32: "She was in . . . my heart." "He . . . wasn't afraid of me." Chafe, *Salon*.

p. 33: "For someone . . . that's why." *Living History*, p. 54.

p. 36: "She was . . . organized." Tumulty, *Time*.

## Chapter 4

p. 37: "I knew . . . without him." *Living History*, p. 70.

p. 42: "No . . . anyway." Ibid., p. 69.

p. 43: "So now . . . by myself." Ibid., p. 74.

p. 48: "I learned . . . my maiden name." Ibid., p. 91.

p. 54: "wife and friend . . . country." http://www.c-span.org/video/?21803-1/governor-bill-clinton-dar-presidential-campaign-announcement.

## Chapter 5

p. 55: "Buy one, get one free." *Living History*, p. 105.

p. 55: "the country ready for the future." Ibid., p. 99.

p. 58: "You're looking . . . other." "You know . . . don't vote for him!" Ibid., p. 107.

p. 59: "Comeback Kid." Ibid., p. 108.

p. 60: "The Economy, Stupid." Miller, *Newsweek*.

p. 61: "I don't care what . . . as my wife!" *Woman in Charge*, p. 205.

p. 61: "You know . . . I can tell you." Ibid., p. 206.

p. 62: "experimented with . . . didn't try it again." Dockterman, *Time*.

# SOURCE NOTES

## Chapter 6

p. 66: "There is nothing wrong . . . right with America." First Inaugural Address of William J. Clinton, January 20, 1993. Library of Congress.

p. 66: "Let's come together . . . for their country." Hillary's speech to the American Medical Association, June 13, 1993.

p. 68: "Welcome to your new house." *Woman in Charge*, p. 235.

p. 68: "the best public housing." www.whitehousehistory.org.

p. 69: "transformed . . . for the balls." *Living History*, p. 126.

p. 69: "Is Hillary beautiful tonight, or what?" The 1993 Inaugural Ball Compilation. https://www.youtube.com/watch?v=Zjk7lMcuZkc.

p. 70: "an unpaid . . . her husband." *The First Ladies Fact Book*, p. 587.

p. 72: "A lot of the mistakes . . . so tired." Drew, *On the Edge*, p. 37.

p. 74: "I smoothed . . . to him." *Living History*, p. 156.

p. 76: "as an American citizen . . . of her nation." Ibid., p. 189.

p. 80: "It is time . . . trying to silence our words." Ibid., p. 305.

p. 80: "may have . . . in public life." *New York Times,* September 6, 1995.

p. 81: "We share . . . families as well." *Living History*, p. 304.

## Chapter 7

p. 84: "Progress . . . values." Democratic National Convention, 1996.

p. 86: "great story . . . president." *Woman in Charge*, p. 498.

p. 87: "No one understands me better." *Living History*, p. 75.

p. 88: "the politics of personal destruction." CNN, December 19, 1998.

## Chapter 8

p. 90: "I suppose . . . me?" Adam Nagourney, *New York Times,* July 8, 1999.

p. 93: "I intend to be . . . hearing about." Ibid.

p. 93: "HRC Speedwagon." *New York Post,* September 8, 2000.

p. 94: "insane process." Diane Kincaid Blair papers, July 28, 1993.

p. 94: "My God . . . so easy!" *For Love of Politics,* p. 405.

p. 96: "Sixty-two counties . . . here we are!" http://news.bbc.co.uk/2/hi/americas/1014007.stm, November 8, 2000.

p. 98: "A workhorse, not a show horse." *Woman in Charge,* p. 548.

p. 100: "will now . . . wrath of our country." *Her Way,* p. 230.

pp. 101–2: "Obviously . . . that way." *Woman in Charge,* p. 549.

**Chapter 9**

p. 103: "I'm in. And I'm in to win." *The Washington Post,* January 21, 2007.

p. 103: "I'm . . . with America." https://www.youtube.com/watch?v=zz1wwhyVOXU.

p. 105: "politics of hope." Transcript, *The Washington Post,* July 27, 2004.

p. 110: "Maybe . . . don't like me." *Game Change,* p. 7.

p. 110: "Well, that hurts . . . that bad." "You're likable enough, Hillary." Debate transcript, *New York Times,* January 5, 2008.

p. 111: "Making change . . . deliver change!" Ibid.

pp. 111–12: "I just . . . to decide." Breslau, *Newsweek.*

p. 113: "pretended to cry." William Kristol on *Fox News,* January 9, 2008. http://mediamatters.org/research/2008/01/09/ny-times-new-columnist-kristol-said-clinton-won/142090.

p. 113: "played the female victim." Dowd, *New York Times,* January 9, 2008.

p. 113: "it took a president." Smith, *Politico,* January 7, 2008.

p. 115: "[We must] take our energy . . . eighteen million cracks in it." Transcript, *New York Times,* June 7, 2008.

p. 116: "Every moment . . . forward." Ibid.

**Chapter 10**

p. 117: "Now . . . leaders." HRC en route to Tokyo, February 15, 2009. Overview of trip to Asia. http://www.state.gov/secretary/20092013clinton/rm/2009a/02/117345.htm.

p. 117: "When . . . say yes." *Hard Choices,* p. 18.

p. 120: "Hello! Hello!" *The Secretary,* p. 11.

p. 120: "This is going to be a great adventure!" *New York Times,* January 22, 2009. http://thecaucus.blogs.nytimes.com/2009/01/22/secretary-of-state-clinton-arrives-at-foggy-bottom/?_r=0.

p. 121: "choosing the right combination of tools . . . for each situation." *Hard Choices,* p. 31.

p. 122: "We do see Asia as part of America's future." HRC en route to Tokyo, February 15, 2009. Overview of trip to Asia. http://www.state.gov/secretary/20092013clinton/rm/2009a/02/117345.htm.

p. 123: "People who think . . . prosperity." HRC, Seoul, South Korea, February 20, 2009. www.state.gov/secretary/20092013clinton/rm/2009a/02/119428.htm.

p. 127: "We came, we saw, he died." HRC, October 20, 2011. www.cbsnews.com.

p. 127: "I sat by her bedside . . . I became." *Hard Choices,* p. 487.

pp. 129–30: "We will . . . undaunted." *HRC,* p. 301.

p. 131: "Benghazi flu." Ibid., p. 341.

p. 132: "misleading the American public." Benghazi hearings, transcript, www.cnn.com.

p. 132: "With all due respect . . . best information." Ibid.

p. 133: "Ultimately . . . inexcusable." Ibid.

p. 134: "Part of our bond . . . thick skins." January 27, 2013. *60 Minutes* transcript, www.hillaryclintonquarterly.com.

# SOURCE NOTES

**Chapter 11**

p. 135: "Wife, mom ... TBD ..." Twitter @HillaryClinton, June 10, 2013.

p. 135: "They throw ... standing." Iowa Democratic Presidential Town Hall, Drake University, January 25, 2016.

p. 136: "beaches ... speeches." *Harper's Bazaar,* February 14, 2011.

p. 139: "Will I run ... decided yet." *Hard Choices,* p. 595.

p. 139: "very combative ... experience." Pilkington, *The Guardian.*

p. 140: "While I was ... passionate about." Elliot, www.dailymail.com.

p. 141: "Looking back ... that way." *The Guardian,* March 10, 2015.

p. 143: "I'm running ... this journey." *New York Times,* April 12, 2015.

p. 144–45: "America's ... not stopping now." HRC announcement speech, June 13, 2015, Roosevelt Island, NY. *Time* Magazine.

p. 149: "most likely ... spouse." Bill Clinton stumps for HRC in first 2016 campaign trail appearance, CNN, October 24, 2015.

p. 151: "I stand ... entire life." HRC, Des Moines, Iowa. CNN, February 2, 2016.

**Author's Note**

p. 152: "the story of America ... continues today." *New York Times,* April 12, 2015.

p. 154: "I challenge ... stand up for themselves." Van Meter, *Vogue,* December 2009.

p. 154: "I wonder who is me? ... famously." Hillary Rodham letter, March 1, 1968, quoted by Sheehy, *Hillary's Choice,* p. 61.

# INDEX

# INDEX

**177**

# INDEX

# INDEX

**181**

# INDEX